WAKE UP!
Rise & Shine

Bo Stehmeier

I want to THANK Mel,

I think we should all say THANK YOU more to Mel!

TABLE OF CONTENTS

LETS BEGIN...

I am eccentric… apparently!

What you are about to read and hopefully follow through on is pretty eccentric too!

When did my love affair with eccentricity begin? Well, I think it was at the age of ten that I was fully awakened to my "specialness". I was living with my parents and two older sisters in Kenya. I can remember it vividly: a period where I had more twigs in my hair than teeth in my mouth, footwear was an enigma, and I was more fluent in dog than any other of the many languages presented to me.

It was also a time when I began to transition physically and mentally from childhood to adolescence. For me, it was a time of double transformation because at that point, my parents were relocating to South Africa, but my sisters decided to move to Europe instead.

So there we were — a household of five now downsized to three, moving to a new country. For me, it was a transformation on many different levels. The new kid on a new block, in a new school without friends and without my sisters for company whilst at the same time transitioning into a young man.

A perfect storm really — every therapist's dream!

South Africa was a deeply scarred and divided country, just emerging from the ravages of apartheid at that time and dragging with it a long history of the brutality of colonialism. And there I was: ten years old, plunged into the deeply entrenched values of South African suburbia, hearing strange languages, wearing a formal school uniform, navigating the intricate system of racial divides and feeling somewhat lost. It was worlds away from the freedom of the outdoors I'd known in Kenya and the Mowgli-type childhood I'd enjoyed there for eight years.

Thus began the long and painful reshaping to fit in with the expected norms and standards. Suddenly I was expected to wear proper lace-up shoes and socks, excel academically and shine at outdoor sports. Socially, kids were expected to be seen but not heard, while parents vied to see whose offspring held the most extra-curricular achievements. Life was rigid: right or wrong, black or white – with no in-between in every sense.

Boy, it was going to be a rough ride for a person like me!

I couldn't fit in! Where in Nairobi I had grown up on acres of land, enjoying life much like a feral kid, barefoot with a great love of animals and running around under open skies, this new lifestyle didn't work for me. I quickly developed body rashes from the polyester uniform and was called names for hanging out with people of other races and color. Academic schooling and sports weren't my thing either. Severely dyslexic with poor coordination, I was not exactly the dream scholar. What I wanted most was to release my bottled-up creativity and to run free with the animals.

My only achievement that was worth discussing at my parent's 19th hole was getting a place in the school swimming team for breaststroke. Unfortunately, no self-respecting colonial African boy wanted to be recognized for their breaststroke swimming skills back then. To compensate for this disappointment, I put all my energy into art, theater, fish tanks and ponds. I had also accumulated a vast dinosaur collection that I took into the garden to create a photo-story along the lines of 'Jurassic Park'. Again nothing that had doctor, lawyer or rocket scientist written all over it!

It's easy to see that growing up, I was the odd one out. Today it's more acceptable to say so, but in South Africa, in the 1990s there was only mainstream — or no stream at all! The result was — BINGO – a royal flush of questionable self-value and personal struggles. To add to that, my initiation into manhood came via the German conscription, the compulsory military service at the age of 21. I was assigned as a tank driver for twelve months and spent most of that time based in a desolate and frozen part of the world, also lovingly referred to as White Russia. It was an immense, and much needed eye-opener in my life with sufficient trauma attached to keep me addicted to the world of self-help for years to come.

Although the early years of my upbringing and transition into manhood were very colorful and somewhat unusual in comparison to the average kid raised in the Western culture, many other people had their own growing up pains, I certainly wasn't alone in my struggles. That's how I accepted it at least, until years later when my own son turned ten.

Although slightly different, I could see a little version of me coming up the ranks. And in my daughter, I also saw much of myself in her growing personality and being.

It was then that I made a commitment that their journey to adolescence was going to be a more guided one.

WHY YOU NEED TO READ
THIS BOOK (NOW)!

Congratulations on taking the time to read this far, and I hope you will continue (you won't regret it)!

Do you have kids and want them to navigate life better? Or do you want your own inner kid to be happier in today's rat race?

Maybe you have a sense of "this can't be it; surely there's more?"

Yes?

Well, then you're in for a good ride!

Here's why I've written this book:

1. We need to wake up, and fast — as a species, as a society, and especially as men.

2. We deserve to wake up because we're currently missing the point and have become a miserable society. This is something I want my kids to avoid; I want them to be

awakened from a young age and avoid sleepwalking through life at any stage.

3. We need practical steps guiding us on how all of this can be done so that anybody can put points 1 and 2 into practice whilst still dealing with the toil of daily life.

4. Consider this as a modern initiation guide written for those of you who want to wake up to what gives you deep joy, and to make sure that those young people who are still awakened through innocence don't fall asleep as they greet adulthood.

Allow me to give you more insight into why I wrote this book:

My son turned ten recently, and I realized that he's on the brink of transformation into manhood. I definitely wanted him to be more prepared for it than I ever was. So I took a couple of steps back and looked at my life. And as I was doing this my life unraveled much more than I'd bargained for. GREAT! So I spent months researching my own hits and misses and also delved deep into my personal treasure trove of self-help tools. I really leaned into life and looked up people who I believed could become a North Star for my kids. During this time of reflection and research, most of the forests on the planet had caught fire, the USA was Trumping, the UK was Brexiting and as if that wasn't enough, the COVID-19 virus hit the scene. There was a perfect backdrop for what really looked to become a dystopian future. And this is what I realized:

1. Time isn't on our side! We have to wake up NOW and give hope to existing and future generations by extinguishing the flames engulfing our planet. While we're ignorantly sleepwalking through our existence, we don't realize that we're to blame for all the destruction.

2. We deserve to wake up to our unique purposes within our communities, as it's the only guarantee of reaching prolonged and sustainable levels of flow; the mother of joy.

3. Re-discovering and re-building a new intergenerational community value system is within our reach and capability. We have the potential to rebuild a more sustainable world.

This book serves as an annual manual to help guide you on your individual awakening. By re-connecting your mind to your body and soul, you will discover your own gifts and find your unique purpose within our community. You will unearth your already existing innate tribe and your personal sphere of influence that embodies the cascading potential to inspire change at a profound systemic level.

Young adults, parents, educators and leaders should use the simple structures in this book to help instill values, purpose and inspire change to ensure the next generation is better equipped for what is bound to become a very bumpy ride ahead. These concepts draw from a tapestry of contemporary science, psychology as well as ancestral teachings. Through accessible language and inspiring symbols, this guide shows you how to sow the seeds of intergenerational transformation (without a budget!). Even the smallest steps taken by you today can become the new growth of tomorrow, so be the change you want to see!

Before we begin, I want to apologize in advance!

a) I believe that all of this stuff is relatively easy and should be written in a conversational tone. I don't want to scare people off with over laboring language often found in this type of literature. Accessibility and making it part of every community language is critical here. So what's about to follow might seem jovial at times; trust me that isn't the intention.

b) Some areas might come across overtly expressive through squiggles, graphs and loud language. Welcome to what goes on in my head! No, seriously, 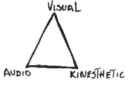 it's proven that we learn by absorbing information in very different ways: auditory, visual and kinesthetic. So this book ticks a lot of the first two boxes whilst the exercises and the Borealis website help for kinesthetic information uptake.

c) Why so esoteric/hippie? You might start asking why use forests and animals, etc. as references. My research very clearly shows that we still have a strong linage that predates the patriarchal systems and the religions they introduced. It's all scattered like Easter eggs throughout our idioms, analogies, fairytales, seasonal festivals and much more. Having survived the test of time, I thought using that kind symbolism to pass on the messages of this book would be incredibly handy, especially when wanting to communicate across generations. My kids took to it like ducks to water.

d) This guide is written in such a way that all you need is a pen, paper and the most valuable element — time — to complete your journey. Everything is kept at a very DIY level. And here's the good news — the solution is within you.

I may not be a guru or an expert, but I've been known for coaching people after a few sherries in the pub. Some of my so-called friends were kind enough to coin the phrase "Oh no, were you Boached last night?" Anyway, I want this guide to have a particular pub feel because that is where I do some of my best work!

So, let's get cracking!

Grab a pen and paper, and if you feel like it, a cold beer!

Let's get started! Let's start writing a new narrative for our future!

THE DEATH OF PATRIARCHY AND THE INITIATION OF THE NEW MAN-CHILD

So, as I said, my son turned ten last year (how time flies) — on the brink of progress towards maturity, at the beginning of the coming-of-age phase of his life. That got me remembering my own experience of transitioning from childhood to adolescence and early manhood. As memories of my own experiences began to flood my mind, I knew that I didn't want these developmental years to leave him feeling confused and isolated. I also wanted to spare him years of self-questioning. I wanted to draw from my life experiences to help guide my kids through this crucial phase. The more I thought about it, the more consumed I became by the notion that we should have a rite of passage to pass on to our kids so that they know what life is really about. But what is life really about and what did I have to offer them? I began researching my linage to identify the values I wanted to pass on to my kids. Reaching out to my parents, the conversations very quickly turned to the World Wars and how they had scarred the world and especially the generations that grew up at that time in Europe. Although set with some decent core values like strength and stoicism, the World War II wrapper was so out of context it wasn't easy to translate into today's setting without alienating my kids before we even got started. As I delved deeper, I realized that my colorful upbringing left me without a well-established linage, per se. I began to doubt if I had actually transitioned in the first place? My wife quite likes to remind me that I have a 'Peter Pan' complex and that it wasn't in her life plan to get married to a middle-aged man-child! Man-child — yes, I could identify with that! On reflection, I did go through some kind of ritual transition, having served a year in the military. It was a shuddering and challenging experience, so it must count for something, right? But surprisingly, after my World War conversation with my parents, I didn't think that my infantry tank wisdom had a suitable essence or edge for it to be introduced to my kids at such a tender age. If I couldn't draw from my own linage then maybe I should use my colorful upbringing to my advantage! The Maasai people of East Africa give their kids a centuries-old coming-of-age ceremony during which the community celebrate the transition as a gift to the tribe as well as offering the young people the honor of taking up responsibilities within the tribe. There were tales that back in the day, part of the rite of passage to manhood and becoming a warrior required young men to survive by themselves in the bush and only come back once they were capable of cutting off the tail of a lion. An interesting and bulletproof approach, but not something that seems appropriate for 2021 and beyond. I mean, the only lion my kids are aware of is the Lion King — so I'll pass on that one, thank you very much!

Still, what could I do and where was our community to help me figure this out?

In this day and age, people create a sense of community from social media interaction and gaining followers. The reality is that an online community isn't a real community that offers guidance and genuine interaction at an intergenerational level. I mean, I do like the idea of kids learning to fend for themselves but thanks to our failed sense of community this seems dangerous. If I push my kids out of the front door to fend for themselves, who do they turn to? It could mean handing them straight over to gangs and drug dealers that run the streets. *Another pass, thanks!*

Maybe I could soften the survival blow and put them in charge of ordering a KFC family bucket at a drive-through (with my money of course) to make them feel genuinely independent? Maybe that could be the most practical coming-of-age gesture?

My search for options continued!

While all of this was going on in my mind, history was repeating itself in our family. We moved to another country in Europe, and whilst it wasn't as geographically extreme as my move as a child, it was still a significant change for all of us. Moving countries during the 2020 global pandemic made the transition feel especially edgy. I worried about my kids, seeing that they were around the same age I was when my family relocated. With this being my 8th country move and all, I have excellent experience at hand to help my kids navigate the change, but that's all I had. I felt I needed something that was more deeply rooted for the biological changes that lay ahead of them.

Continued research came up with very little. I considered religion, but the protestant route seemed as far removed from reality as the Maasai lion hunt; it wouldn't work, so I had to delve deeper. Apart from converting to Judaism, where a rite of passage into manhood is still followed, or using the rituals of far-flung tribes that make no sense in our WEIRD societies, there were no obvious options.

"What are WEIRD societies?" you ask. **Western, Educated, Industrialized, Rich and Democratic – WEIRD. I love it!** Regrettably, not my creation, but I do love it because this so-called "tribe" has started feeling as weird as it sounds. It turns out that my family is part of the WEIRD tribe that makes up one-eighth of the world population. A tribe that's very influential when it comes to global decision-making, but couldn't organize a piss-up in a brewery when it comes to self-reflection and showing responsibility.

Back to the drawing board! Possibly I could start exposing my son to the ten years of self-help that I'd sucked up in my attempts to fix my bumpy transition? Once again I dived down the rabbit hole of the Eckhart Tolle's of this world to see what could form part of my kids' initiation… and it was then that it suddenly hit me! All these books, podcasts, TedEX talks, gurus, yogis and world religions that I had been devouring had the same link at their core: ritual and storytelling. The ancient art of passing on wisdom and knowledge that's still practiced today by many remote and ancient tribes and their linages.

While all of this was going on in my mind, outside the Amazon rainforests, flames were consuming California and Australia. Trump was throwing his toys out of the pram on one side of the Atlantic, Brexit was in full swing on the other, and we were changing countries. As if that wasn't enough, COVID-19 arrived and devastatingly smashed through global populations. I know I'm repeating myself… but it's essential to repeat it to really bring home how broken the WEIRD tribe had become and that it will be our tribe's name on the bill when the time comes to pay up (with borrowed money no doubt!).

All of this spurred on my innate urgency to derive a coming-of-age plan to equip my kids with the right tools to navigate what appears to be a very uncertain future. If you listen to some glass-half-empty experts, they predict that today's kids could be the last generation on this planet. WOW!

But now I had a lead, a connection. So I pulled up my socks, got off my arse, read, listened, gathered, learned and used my god given intuition (yes exactly that skill that made me the last to get picked during football matches in colonial Africa), and pulled everything together. No stone was left unturned in my quest to understand this WEIRD tribe we belong to and where it's heading and how we can possibly fix it!

As I type this, I'm sitting in Lapland having spent a whole week with a Nordic shaman learning about connection from him.

He's been teaching me the ancient ways of living in alignment with the earth. I had flashbacks of my Mowgli-esque upbringing, and my inner kid began to unfold in front of me. The shaman spent most of his time teaching me how one can come *"home to one's self"*.

What an odd concept, I thought, *aren't we home anyway?*

And before I knew it, yet another rabbit hole revealed itself to me; so up I pulled on my green Peter Pan man-child tights, and I jumped in ● ! (You will see these symbols appear now and then! They symbolize rabbit holes that invite you to dive deeper into the subject being covered. Enjoy!).

What I found was totally mind-blowing… hardly anybody in the WEIRD tribe is truly emotionally at home!

Whilst rechecking my head for clever knock-knock jokes to go with this new revelation, it became very clear to me…

… I mean we, the WEIRD tribe, are transitioning out of a hyper-patriarchal world that has profoundly shaped us for the last 6,000 years or so! It's been era characterized by fierce masculine energy expressed through aggression, control and ownership. It translated into our building empires, condoning slavery, creating currency, mass religious conversion, industrialization, wars, and even getting us to the moon and back. The energies associated with masculinity are linear, structured, protective, forceful, logical, focused, independent and disciplined. These values became highly revered and built into every nook and cranny of the storylines and narrative that has created the lineage of the WEIRD tribe.

These are the values that have ultimately gotten us to the civilization we live in today. But as with anything extreme in life, it comes at a price. You see, to own and control something you need to separate yourself from it. Over thousands of years of patriarchy, we've managed to separate humans from nature, ourselves from animals and men from women. We're separated by geography, religion, race, age, education, income, sexuality, political views — the list goes on and on and on. We've even succeeded in separating "me" from "we", where the needs of the individual are more important than those of the group.

Why is that?

Simply because the patriarchal commodity-driven economy benefits more from you being a separated, vulnerable individual. Being isolated from the herd makes you much more fragile, and you start turning to the system for the support you'd innately get from your own flock. Living in alienated nuclear families, we are dependent on the system for our housing, childcare, schooling systems, nursing homes, health care, and life/health insurances. In our isolation, we turn to multi-million industries built around us to have fun, find love or to look good so that we can fit in and get approval from our estranged tribe. Needless to say, we pay for accessibility of these false sustentation systems that are all driven by profit and owned by a small handful of super-rich capitalists. At the same time, we slave away to earn some money to afford the basics in life. We've even gone so far that we define our life purpose and ourselves by how much money we make.

Sounding overly dramatic, of course, but I'm trying to make a point here!

And the scariest new frontier of attack, the last sacred bastion whereby we're separating mind, from body? In the relentless pursuit for growth, the latest business frontier feeding our commodity- and consumption-based economy has moved on from preying on our disposable income to also harvesting our disposable time! We're all stuck behind electronic devices that demand our attention in exchange for cheap and quick dopamine kicks! Our brains are literally circumnavigating their keeper, the body, and plugging directly into the internet in search of joy. So much so that many people are starting to question what is real and what isn't. Daniel Schmachtenberger believes we're already steeped in the third World War. A war that we might not recognize as war because no tanks are driving around or bombs are getting dropped, but blurring the lines of what is and isn't real is the trenches in which the current global war is being fought. ● 'War on Sensemaking', Daniel Schmachtenberger

Okay, before you start self-harming, I also found very encouraging signs of change… BIG change!

As with any pendulum, once it's reached its most extreme point, it starts to swing back. After 6,000 years of patriarchal ownership and control, there are obvious signs of a swing into a space of collaborative structures with a more collective thought process on a truly global scale. Signs of this change are epitomized by names like Jacinda Adern, Barack Obama, Angela Merkel, Greta Thunberg, Nelson Mandela, Mahatma Gandhi, and many more. And there are also great signs in technology including systems like crypto, blockchain and other emerging systems to ensure personal control and transparency.

Of course, it goes without saying, change and transformation don't come without growing pains. The recent street riots and hashtag movements are all an expression of deep trauma that's finally rising to the surface, finding expression and getting heard. There are also deeply engrained systems and powers that don't want to see these changes, though. The (former) Trump government and Brexit supporters being clear examples.

The burning question: Is the pendulum stoppable or possibly too slow? Time is not on our side. We can't expect meaningful systemic change to happen in the small amount of time we have left to turn this nightmare around.

From early childhood, values and concepts of the WEIRD tribe were instilled in us. And at that time we didn't have the awareness or know any differently so we just accepted them. Patriarchal ideas of separation allowed us to put ourselves at the center of our own universe, blurring our appreciation of dependency on others, the world and its systems. Like bloodhounds, we are trained from a young age to follow the money.

We live in an unnatural state. Think about it! We didn't earn any of the primary things that keep us alive, or that makes life worth living. We didn't earn the life-giving air we breathe, the water that maintains life, nor being born. We didn't earn our parents, love, friendship, laughter, the weather, the earth beneath our feet or the rivers and oceans. How often do we truly appreciate the sun and the moon that rise and set daily, sustaining all life forms?

So, on some level, we should all be born with an immense sense of gratitude, knowing life itself is a gift that we didn't earn. But here's the twist. If you know that you've received a gift, then the natural response should be gratitude and a desire to give back. American author, Charles Eisenstein calls it the Gift Economy. In a gift economy, the more you give, the richer you are. ● **'Gift Economy', Charles Eisenstein**

This concept is in striking contrast with our modern-day money economy where we're all in competition to have the most zeros attached to our bank balance. The gift economy is about finding yourself and how you can contribute value to your immediate society and the people around you. In this way, we foster communal bonding and security. As you offer value to people, they recognize it and are grateful. In turn, they're willing to repay you reciprocally. Cycles of mutual giving and receiving without competition or comparison. Without gifts, the idea of a community is dead!

(Yup, this is the moment where a lot of you might say... "Good god what a hippie!")

Welcome to the 21st century, where society is becoming more and more monetized by the day. Communities get moved and homes demolished for industry. Forests get destroyed for expansion. Commercial farming treats animals as commodities, genetically modified crops kill indigenous insects and plant life to ensure maximum harvest yields. Financially it makes sense, but a thriving commodity-driven economy is devoid of community. The longing for a community often gets sensed as a deep yearning — a void that can't be filled. But the system doesn't allow you to fill that void because it would rather sell services and things to you that pretend to fill that void in the form of institutions, personal care, insurances, hedonistic nightlife, or stuff to fill up your homes. So people turn to consumerism, substances and other unhealthy habits to fill the emptiness. But what they're actually longing for is a place where they can find an identity within themselves and people they can call their own. Unfortunately, genuine community can't just be an add-on to a monetized life, even if social media and gaming networks are trying their darn hardest to make us believe that.

It's time to WAKE UP: we need each other! Humans aren't created to survive alone. We have a desire to share our time, our journey and our gifts. Money, however, is frequently a barrier keeping us from living our best lives. How many times have you thought "oh, I'd love to try that"? Then it dawns on you, "can I afford it?" "Is it practical?" "Where does it fit in my budget and most importantly, do I have time for it?"

Most are yet to find their calling because they're caught up in the money-making rat race, and even if they have an idea they regularly find money is an obstacle to complete self-expression. In reality, money stops them from finding themselves.

Sadly, an unfound person is a person who doesn't know the destination they're navigating towards. Considering the stormy seas that face us, you need to have your own navigational equipment well-adjusted before you head into those rough waters.

While money remains a crucial element of our society, we must loosen its grip and break down the barriers it places on our living a fuller life. Again I say, we need to wake up! In truth, time is not on our side. Virtually every coin you spend is most likely supporting a business whose bottom line has zero interest in giving back to the world or its environment. We are controlled by money, and men specifically are the most deeply entranced by its allure. Possibly it's the result of primal societies where men went out to hunt while the women gathered. Did hunting evolve into "bringing home the bacon", where our prime reason for existence is to be doomed to the hamster wheel of economic growth and cash generation? Living in a patriarchal society has our masculine role, narrative and gender so intrinsically linked and intertwined with the money-making machine that it's virtually impossible to see past it.

It would seem that men have the longest journey ahead of them when it comes to transformation and identifying their role and narrative in the new, more collaborative world. While it might be a touch too late for me, I want my kids, and especially my son, to see and explore other options that lie ahead for him that aren't part of the world as we know it. Options that are better suited to our innate abilities and therefore allow us to align our lives closer to our true purpose. I'm aware that right now is not the time for men to have their moment. There are too many other lineages of trauma that need to be unraveled, healed and repositioned, such as #blacklivesmatter and #metoo to mention just two. All I'm saying is that that the initiation into the 'new masculine' still lies ahead of us, and with #heforshe, the first slow baby steps have begun... but there's a long, long old journey ahead of us.

But as they say, each journey starts with a single step, and that's why you are here, and it's my job to ensure that you will take that first step.

Time flies at warp speed these days. Before you know it, you'll be planning for retirement!

Flash-forward for a moment: when you sit down and reflect on your life, would you say that you've lived your purpose or, instead, saved for retirement? In your later years, would you draw energy from your best career moves, or from having added value to your community that still sustains you in the autumn of your life? Would you say that you made the best of your true potential?

Back to the rabbit hole!

When I finally poked my head out of the last rabbit hole, I had more clarity on what needs to happen.

We are progressively destroying our increasingly over-populated planet, and our wellbeing is suffering. The myth we're fed that acquiring an ever-increasing amount of money and material stuff will bring us joy is just that — a myth. Never before have people been so rich in resources and lacking in genuinely satisfying options! Being deeply rooted in our community will make us less vulnerable to the alluring taunts of our commodity-driven society. A society that happily rapes and pillages to ensure bottom-line growth. And it has created a mass of people who see the badge of financial success as a sign of personal achievement, wellbeing and assured happiness. GDP is still the international measure of the success of a nation whilst their statistics around mental health, poverty and crime paint an entirely different picture.

This guide will help us break this cycle. "The whole is greater than the sum of its part" truly encompasses the value that needs to consciously and genuinely become instilled to avoid our looming extinction. Community is at the center of our wellbeing as a species. If we come together as a tribe and pool our resources, we'd find a unique bountiful richness both individually and within our still existing ecosystems.

Paradoxically the more we invest in our tribes, the more we reap the rewards of a profound sense of purpose and flow, leading to more sustainable joy and fuller happiness. It's here we discover the key to free us from the chains that bind us. Nurturing our innate connectivity from macro to micro and back again is at the center of this work.

I knew that at a micro level, I needed to help my kids go through their initiation to adulthood. Likewise, I'm also painfully aware that society as a whole is going through it's own coming-of-age process. And within that, men have the most prolonged transition ahead of them.

My focus is on men here and that might get peoples' backs up. But being one myself, and knowing my son needs to recognize what it means to be a man in the next chapter of his life, and hopefully the new society that will come with it, this work has a natural leaning towards the masculine at times. Coming out of an extremely patriarchal era, the value and meaning of what it means to be a man needs to be redefined. And as the two are so innately intertwined, it's an intensely complicated process.

It should be noted that while this guide does have a leaning towards the masculinity (the masculine energy within anything, including women — Thatcher being a prime example) it remains completely applicable to all genders and all ages: everyone needs to get on board with this journey, discovering our true purpose, if we are to change things on the global scale that's so desperately needed.

Now I am no psychic and won't pretend that I have any idea what this new world, post-transition will look like. What I do know, however, is that our current WEIRD lives are not serving us well. What we've become is a blueprint of what the consumption economy wants us to be. It's time to rewire the system from within. By staying within the confines of the system, we'll never be able to guide change. We need to take life by the horns, take back control of the steering wheel and come to be the cause of things, not the effect. Now's the time to discover who we are, what makes us tick, who matters to us and how we can help serve them with the purpose we've been given.

It time to come home!

It can be argued that it took us 6,000 years (painful as they were) to get us to a point in our global evolution as a species that we are so interconnected through business and the information highways that we can now finally take a truly global step, together, to make this transition as a species. It's something that even 50 years ago wouldn't have been possible. So it's not about shunning the current system and technology but actually using it as a backbone for this forthcoming transition.

This is our transition, our coming-of-age journey. I'll undergo it with my kids, as a man, as the community and as the society for a new future.

And here you have the blueprint! Ballsy statement I know… but hear me out!

I've compiled all my rabbit hole notes and drawings into this this project consisting of a website and two items pretending to be books.

The original title was "The World According To Bo, The Mumbling Memories Of A Middle-Aged Man- Kid" — but thanks to the input of some very attentive friends I promised to compile the book in a way that can be shared more widely. This book is part of a guide and fun website that all encompass Borealis — a whole world of self-discovery.

It endeavors to help guide you on your journey to finding home, your true purpose and not the purpose that got sold to you. It will help you focus on what you discover and convert awareness into intention that can be executed through easy plans that you can set yourself. **This isn't an anarchist guide to middle finger society, as quite frankly we don't have the time for teenage moments.** It's about ensuring that the micro-decisions you make daily align with the true direction you should be on. Rome wasn't built in a day, and I'm very aware that you'll get pulled off this project more frequently than you might like, but don't worry – it's has been compiled with precisely that in mind.

Okay, enough talking about it. Let's step to the ledge and JUMP!

CHAPTER

1

MIRROR, MIRROR ON THE WALL AND THE PILOT

This is the most crucial chapter you'll ever read in your LIFE!

You'll either leave this chapter with a "what's the biggy?" or a "Holyshit!" The answer will be defined by how ready you are for your journey.

You're about to meet the operating system behind the operating system... so I hope you're feeling bright-eyed and bushy-tailed and bursting with playful enthusiasm!

If not, put the book down until you're feeling more enthusiastic.

I remember the first time my kids said, "My dad loves taking selfies!" They weren't lying; I do like taking selfies, especially with groups of people. I've become quite a pro. My friends have gone as far as calling them Bo-selfies. They even send me pics taken when hanging out with their friends so that

I can check the quality, style and technique! ☺

Many people are very quick to judge this activity, and boy they do, but it's never stopped me. You see for me, it's the moment I step out of my daily autopilot mode and into the awareness that connects me to the bigger questions in life. This photographic ritual is prompted by a constant inner dialog seeking macro awareness for myself. I want to create a photo diary of where I am, who I'm with and why I have the urge to capture the moment for all eternity.

Although often judged as a narcissistic exercise, to me it's more about capturing milestones of life. Sometimes I'm also very aware that something needs to be a Bo-selfie moment because of the value the day carries in the greater scheme of life. What I love about this activity is that it's not only a moment in time for me but it also secretly reflects back on everyone and everything in the picture with me. It shows that they're an essential part of my emotional landscape — and part of my camera roll... my never-ending camera roll! In my never-ending camera roll, I take pictures of anything that really evokes a thought process, a memory or something humorous. So you can say it's a bit of a photo diary

Over the last ten years, I have captured over 18,000 pictures with my phone (and that number is heavily edited). A lot of people tend to paint technology with the devil's brush. Still, I genuinely believe that with the right intent and awareness, we can count ourselves as a very fortunate generation for being able to have the universe in our pockets.

Now before I go more in-depth into this and risk losing you, please pick up your phone and select video selfie mode. You probably want to do this when you're alone, although it would be highly entertaining if you would do it in public!

Record yourself answering the following five questions, but don't prepare — just jump in! For the less progressive amongst you, doing this in front of a mirror can do the trick too!

(If you don't want to do this then you might as well stop reading here because this is not the right journey for you — harsh but true!)

Ready? Let's go!

1. **Who am I?**
2. **What do I love to do?**
3. **Who do I do it for?**
4. **What do they want or need?**
5. **How do they change as a result?**

Done? Okay then, you can read on (ideally don't replay your responses immediately).

What I want is for you to walk through the different awareness's you had when answering those questions. Slow right down and close your eyes. In your mind's eye recapture the experience from your senses only. Sometimes you might pick up comments in a different voice while recording without realizing it.

Give it a break before you listen to the recording. Envision it and take as much time as you need. Make notes and drawings. Especially focus on where in your body you were most present when you interviewed yourself. If you feel like you can't really focus on it anymore, go back to the recording and with the same state of mind, listen to it again and again and again.

Write down what you felt, saw, heard, maybe even smelt and tasted. If you become aware of another inner voice commenting on the recording, what was the voice that crept in? Listen to the voice, commenting on the answers. Was it male, female, human, did it have an accent? What was the tone, style and speed of the voice? Did it swear, speak with words, a different language, or did it only make sounds? Do you recognize the voice from somewhere?

Welcome to your control center behind your control center. The pilot that whispers into your ear! As the saying goes – "the bad news is time flies, the good news is you are the pilot" — but who is the actual pilot?

Well, there are two pilots. One is the autopilot, and the other is the pilot who takes charge when the autopilot is out of its comfort zone. The reality with humans is that our autopilot is pretty darn amazing! How come? Because the human brain is a very energy-hungry organ and is hardwired to build patterns and routines that can be programmed into autopilot mode and then embedded deeply into your subconscious. Why? Because the less you have to think about anything, the less energy the body wastes on trying to reinvent to navigate activities and challenges in our daily life. Besides energy efficiency, it also allows us to act faster. Back at a primal level, this was super handy when humans still actually needed to run away from their enemy physically.

Some of this hardwiring is still very handy today, like touch-typing right now! But there are many, MANY autopilot reactions we use daily that are questionable. However, they can only be questioned if you switch off the autopilot at times to see if you're really still set on the right course.

Most of the things that motivate us to make decisions were set very early in our childhood when our brain's plasticity, or hunger to learn, was at an all-time high. It's a phase in our development where things like language acquisition are very quickly hardwired deep into the brain. Something else that was hardwired was loads of social and societal conditions. Things like: "winning is important", "boys are good at math", "girls excel in languages", "having a spouse and making a home is a sign of success", and many, many more. When playing back that video, especially your answer to question 4 about what they want or need — that moment is when the pilot is speaking out.

Here we're getting to the crux of this chapter! If we can create a space between having and feeling our emotions and can become aware of the strength of emotions in contrast to what has caused them (down to the root cause if possible), then you're stepping into the pilot that is managing the autopilot. Accessing the cause of our emotions can be done in a split second once we know how.

Eckhart Tolle refers to it as the "all-seeing-eye". The inner eye, the third eye that can witness and remain aware of how our emotions are moving on a spectrum and are aligned with what's happening in our environment. This relationship between the eye, the awareness and the spectrum form 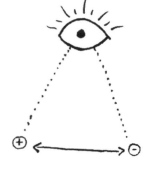 the legendary triangle, an ancient symbol that has many layers of meaning throughout history. It will also create the backbone to visualize some of the critical drivers of the awakening process over the next couple of chapters.

Be prepared to get 'triangled'! All the drawings provided in this book are designed to help you build shortcuts on your path to awakening.

The importance of the eye looking at a spectrum is key because awareness is about measuring the strength of the emotion, what prompted it and if it's in line with the situation or what you stand for or represent. For example, if you're waiting in a long queue in the rain and somebody cuts in, or even worse you get to the front and find they don't take cards and only accept cash, you'll have a fight or flight reaction. You might walk off feeling disgruntled or worse, have an outburst, making harsh remarks (that many people will find hilarious). What happened is that the event triggered a deep-seated autopilot reaction of your perception as to whether the incident was right or wrong.

You see, everything in life is continuously moving on a spectrum without us being able to exert any influence on it... but BOY do we try! Everything in life is dual, has poles, pairs of opposites, like and unlike; they're the same. Opposites are identical in nature but different in the degree of extremes they meet. All truths are but half-truths and somewhere on that spectrum is where we've locked in where we stand. We adopted our position way back when we were still trying to figure out life on this planet. And many of these positions weren't discovered by us, but are the result of social conditioning by our families, friends, culture, education and other external factors. As we grow up, they become so deeply ingrained in our autopilot that it's almost impossible for us to recognize them, never mind question if they're still aligned with who we've become.

To reflect, consider how you answered the question **"who am I"?**

Whose point of view were you expressing and how much of that was you using society's labels that get bandied about on a daily basis and include your job or social standing?

My answer could have sounded something like this:

"Who are you?"

"I'm Bo, married father of two, manager of...."

Or along the lines of:

"I'm Bo — good dot connector who loves going to festivals with my wife. I have a deep passion for all things beer, chicken and doing visual stuff with my kids. My biggest Achilles' heel is writing and my uncontrollable anxiety around extreme introverts".

One of these answers will feel much more substitutable yet easier to target a commodity-driven economy, whilst the other response is uniquely shaped to my reality. It's also more likely to be put forward by people who are part of my community and are more interested in an emotional exchange rather than a commercial exchange. That's how people who aren't commercially interactive with you will probably describe you.

This needs to sink in!

If your own answer was similar to the first one, then you've become more of an imprint of society and its standards. Conversely, if your answer was closer to the latter, then you've started to embrace the version of yourself that truly matters, and you've already started your journey of questioning aspects of your autopilot.

So why is this so important?

Every cause has an effect, and every effect has a cause and if your cause is not true to your core then the effect, the life around you, is not going to materialize in the way you want. Let's say you want a promotion, then that will be your cause — your primary focus, and it will end up with an effect, either positive or negative. The bigger question, however is: Is the promotion actually your real cause? Possibly a more exact cause is that you deserve a promotion and the desire is actually rooted in wanting to be recognized in the organization or receive more respect for the work that you've done. If you don't identify the root cause, gaining the desired effect by being given a promotion will be short-lived. You'll soon you slip back into the same shadows of feeling a lack of respect and attention.

Ultimately, where you put your focus in life is where things will manifest, for good or bad. And because we only have a finite amount of energy and time, we must make decisions from our authentic pilot rather than from our autopilot perspective.

The following chapters will help you uncover your true pilot to know your true identity better and enable you to make decisions that are aligned with who you really are. Your reality is, in fact, negotiable if you start focusing your attention on your new-found awareness.

Life is so full of noise that you can barely hear yourself and your inner voice. Many people spend their entire life trying to find their purpose and accrue enough money for their retirement while remaining stuck on the Monopoly board game of life.

REALITY IS NEGOTIABLE

The more significant part of the self-help industry focuses on precisely these people who around halfway through their life suddenly have a moment where they cannot account for much of what they've done or achieved. They feel as though they've wasted time. Their lives are controlled by their employer, their house is owned by the bank, their kids are being raised by an institution and if they're lucky and have a good job, and then once a year they get to max out their credit card to go on a summer holiday package deal targeted and sold to "I am Bo, a married father of two, manager of..."

Of course, I am exaggerating here to make my point and, yes, I'm known for being a drama queen, but I'm making a fuss in the hope of giving you a glimpse of your autopilot (who at this point might be grumbling in your cognitive background at my statements!)

Early in our lives, we swallowed the proverbial "magic pill", without even knowing that we could question it. Buying into a world where you can find your life purpose by being on someone else's payroll. And the higher you climb in the ranks, the more your purpose grows. Importance and levels of enjoyment are made accessible to you through social esteem and accumulation of material wealth.

Wrong! Money doesn't bring us joy — especially if we don't even have the time to spend it, or even worse, most of it gets eaten up covering the basics of life's necessities. What I find the scariest is that our entire autopilot program, our inner satnav, has been acutely programmed to do just that! We're hard-wired to travel along the conveyor belt of life. And what's even more frightening is the society and institutions that programed us in the past are suddenly realizing that resources in the world and the planet itself are running out. The conveyor belt is starting to come off its wheels and is starting to tear.

That's why we need to wake up our pilot because the journey ahead is about to get bumpy! The looming storms need to be embraced by coherent minds and not 'sheeple'.

I'm not implying that you need to be an anarchist and wash your current lifestyle and career down the drain. Life has happened for good or bad. You're on a journey and the time has come for you to make better micro decisions when you reach the next intersection. The better your micro-decisions are, the greater the positive outcomes on the macro effect will be. And it's our pivotal responsibility that the next generation doesn't even get to see the "magic pill" so that they enter the system wide awake and help rework and reprogram it from within.

This is where TEDx speaker Adam Leipzig and his five questions that I posed at the beginning of this chapter are so incredibly suitable for the awakening up process. They form part of his talk 'How to know your life's purpose in 5 minutes'.

Leipzig made an echoing statement that I'd like to share with you:

"An unexamined life is not worth living."

The daily news is a constant reminder of how broken the external world is. Sadly, the reason for that is because our internal worlds are not in order either, and our attitudes are outdated. Despite so much wrong with the world, the reality is that it's not going to improve anytime soon. In fact, more negativity and disasters will happen day by day, year in, year out. This is the **macro crisis**. Many global as well as local communities want to do something about it. Our lives are more than just ourselves. We should care about other people in other places who are going through struggles that might not be immediately affecting us. However, just like in the plane crash, you need to put on your own oxygen mask first before you can help others.

It's all about "Me first; make me great again!" ☺

The most sustainable way of tackling the big stuff is if you wake up to your own **micro crisis**. These are personal crises relating to our internal struggles and our internal fight for an awakening. Self-realization might take focus and effort, but anyone who can take the reins will triumph over their micro crises.

To rewrite your own narrative, you must start by understanding that reality is negotiable; it's all based on perception. When you judge yourself and others, from whose point of view are you doing this? The truth is, when it comes to intrinsic **micro assessment**, the only **point of view is yours.** This is because nobody knows you better than you know yourself. You are the only expert of your own awareness. Therefore, you must pay close attention to how you judge and from what perception your judgment stems. In truth, when you take people's judgments and comments to heart, you might also end up taking their vile and impure intentions with it. When people make statements about you, are their remarks always sincere? Do they really want to see you prosper or do they just want to mock your deficiencies and with that, reveal their own!?

Sure, there are people whose judgments are pivotal. Your spouse, kids and family; they should know you well enough to keep you on track. However, you should still listen with a filter. Be hyper vigilant! When you or others are passing comments, are the intentions genuine? Or do they just want to get a reaction?

Throughout your journey in life, you will embark on plenty of adventures. And in truth, you are the hero of your own story as well as the one who determines your adventures. All you need is the map that will lead you to the treasures you seek. The role you play in your life adventure and the treasures you unearth are all in your hands. Embrace Eckhart Tolle's all-seeing-eye of awareness and check in on your five senses regularly. Become hyper-aware of the inner voice of your pilot; the more you do, the faster the treasure map will start to unfold in front of you. Become the guru of your own self-awareness. Question if it's my own thought that I am pursuing or the biologically deep-routed groupthink of the sheeple of society. ◉ **Groupthink: A Study in Self Delusion, Christopher Booker**

As with everything in life – only practice makes perfect. That's the reason I've littered this book with weird-looking eyeballs. Whenever you stumble across an eye, I'm asking you to quickly stop, close your eyes, become aware of what your self-broadcast saying and what the emotional weather report is like. As you start listening to this self-broadcast channel, have a bit of fun and give it a name (most likely it already has a name on one of your Spotify playlists).

Since its only practice that achieves perfection, I'll leave you with a gigantic piece of homework. It's not only for this specific chapter, though, it's also in preparation for the chapters to come. When you get to the end of the book, you'll see that the year ahead will be all about you engaging in playful experimentation. Many of you will be feeling resistance to this. Perfect! Lean into the resistance and its energy because it's not resistance that's the enemy; it's the autopilot telling you that you're going off course.

That's exactly the reaction we want – so let's go off course and engage with the safari of life!

P.S. Whatever you do, **don't delete the recording you made at the beginning of the chapter** because we'll go back to it... A LOT!

Homework

Welcome to your resentment therapy session!

As I said earlier, the brain is built to be hardwired for certain things. We have little say as to what the brain decides to hardwire, and some things are already built-in (especially within the pleasure centers). On the most basic level, we have triggers in two most basic behaviors — getting away from a situation and moving towards something we enjoy. During our evolution, something unique happened in our brain; something that enabled us to evolve at speed far greater than any other animal could do in the same space of time. We developed the skill to conceptualize abstract thoughts and space, like "democracy" and "time" itself. It enabled us to pass wisdom and teaching down from one generation to the next, meaning that the future generations didn't have to start from scratch.

Amazing!

What is less remarkable is that we still have hardwired in our brains the instinct to escape from dangers, like the sabre tooth tiger, or to find the sugary ripe fruit to supplement what was back then, a diet low in sugars.

You probably already know where I'm going with this. Our brains' wiring hasn't evolved at the same pace as we have started to take control of the environment around us. The result is that, the WEIRD tribe in particular has become the most deadly and obese predator or enemy, not only to the environment but to ourselves. And not only in our actions but also in our thinking.

So where am I going with this? The brain has a distinct penchant in the wiring towards fight or flight rather than seeking pleasure because it's still geared towards focusing on survival. That means that our brain's focus is towards danger and negativity to ensure survival. Connecting back with our amazing evolutionary steps of being able to actualize abstract thoughts and stories, unfortunately the brain quickly perceives hatred, anger, shame, sadness, rage, disgust and jealousy as emotions similar to the threats posed by, for instance, sabre tooth tigers. Something we need to get away from to ensure basic survival. In other words, if people in your life evoke threatening emotions in you, your brain establishes hardwire patterns to get away from them. If you can't, you start building deep resentment towards them.

There's no better way to start questioning and challenging our autopilot when it comes to our interaction with people. It will also build an excellent foundation for the chapter to follow.

According to science, anyone above the age of 40 should be able to list up to 200 names of people in their life with whom they've repeatedly incurred any of the seven emotions just mentioned . I want you to write the names of these people down and next to their name the emotion or emotions that they triggered in you. And yes, of course, people can appear more than once; it's more about the content than the actual people.

While this might seem like a tall order, I guarantee you that this list will become handy in the ensuing chapters. For the courageous, start a second list of names where you think that you might appear on others peoples emotional trigger list and why!

Don't take this exercise lightly either. Thanks to our brain's superpower we also can relive our past in the now.

Some of you might start derailing while doing this. This project has the capacity to catapult you straight back to the actual moments when the resentment was instilled, resulting in you getting stuck on certain people. Why the hell would I want you to do that? Well, these are the people who set some of your deepest autopilot controls and if you're going to reprogram then see this as your yellow brick road.

So if a person's memory triggers more information than you care to recall, just acknowledge it and give it a star, as a reminder to get back to it. For those of you who get so stuck on that name and can't move on, I invite you to find a chair and place it in front of you. In your mind's eye, imagine that person who's the subject of your resentment sitting in that empty chair. Start vocalizing what's going through your mind. If you're daring enough, explore sitting in the same chair and being on the receiving end of your shouting and ranting.

I know it might sound a bit odd, but it's all part of making your pilot look in the mirror to see who is the fairest in the land! And, as I said, keep the list as it will become your yellow brick road into the forest of self-discovery.

CHAPTER 2

WHO AM I: THE TREE OF LIFE

I love dragons!

And I always have, so I'm more than happy that they're making a comeback in mainstream media in a big way. Many cultural anthropologists believe that dragons and other mythological creatures like unicorns are making a massive return because society has a desire to reconnect with ancient myths that existed before the major religions took over — but that's a whole different book on its own.

So dragons are back, whether in 'Lord of the Rings', 'Game of Thrones', 'Avatar' or my personal favorite, 'How to Train Your

Dragon'. The story mirrors itself: it's about a human having to overcome their own fear of something bigger, more ancient and wiser. And in overcoming this milestone in the fairytale, the next leg of the journey unfolds as you team up with the ancient beast.

Well, we're about to have a very similar moment, so hold on tight...

I want you to use your imagination here. Imagine yourself as the rider of a dragon with not one, but three heads. This is your dragon for life; taming it is always your responsibility, from the day you're born to the day you leave this world. But your dragon isn't very tame, it's determined to do its own thing, making the ride a bumpy one. Each head relates to a specific part of you, so it has a direct effect on your life, that's why taming it is so critical. One head is linked to your mind, another to your heart and the other to your body.

We're all born with an innate inclination to lean towards one of the heads while compensating for not relying very much on the other two. The trick to taming the dragon is to get all three heads in equal alignment so that you can fly off into the sunset and have incredible adventures together.

Might sound easy enough but most of us don't get it right and some aren't even aware of the dragon we're riding. Yet thanks to the tsunami of self-help literature flooding the market over the last

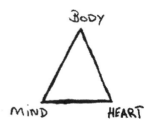

25 years or so, people are becoming aware. They're realizing how much more straightforward, healthier and stable life becomes once the mind, body and heart balance gets addressed.

We're all born with a slight preference (something we'll explore in greater depth in the chapter on the 6-elements), but I am sure you can easily recall your school years. Remember those people who were good at sports, excelled academically, were known for being the life and soul of the party, or those to whom others could pour their hearts out. These all are indicators that they had a leaning towards either mind, body or heart. I grew up with three strong women, my mother and two sisters who were much older than me. Even in that microcosm, I had a reflection of this with one sister clearly being more in her head, the other one was busy with the heart and out socializing, while my mother who had a leaning to her body, was busy with her sporting activities.

Clearly, this oversimplifies a far, far more complex issue, but I want you to understand it (even though it might dent my reputation with my "coachy" friends). I want you to think like a coach – your own life coach. Also, use this dragon scenario when you're working on your resentment list, which you should still be doing. As you bring people to mind, see which way they were leaning: Mind? Body? Heart? And remember everything is on a spectrum…

(… some readers might get irritated by the use of "heart" rather than the classical use of "soul" to close the trinity. The reason for the use of heart is because we are especially focusing on our emotional landscape and in addition, soul can be very abstract for the younger generation).

The reality is that we can all get the balance right and be in all three attributes with very little awareness. In the worst of cases, though, we can become stuck in only one element for most of the time. And because our bodies are so amazing, we can exist living in a single attribute, much like a left-handed person can to learn to write with their right hand. Doing this, though, won't harness the power of your most natural abilities.

In evolutionary terms, it can be argued that the development of the mind is our most uniquely human aptitude and is the only one that should take pride of place at the center of what we do.

Guess what?

It is... and has been for far too long!

That doesn't really surprise me because when you look at a fully formed, healthy baby, it's gifted with a completely functional body and the full house of basic human emotions. It's only due to the hyperactivity in our brains and minds that we learn to walk, speak and define our emotions (and how to best act them out to manipulate our parents).

Over the thousands of years that patriarchy has ruled society, the mind has been celebrated as the most sacred of all attributes, above the body and heart. To prove the point, look at how we subject our offspring to close on 20 years of education that prioritizes and hones the brain's intellect and places little value on embracing emotional or physical intelligence.

You see, the brain is a bit like a new iPhone. You can choose what apps you upload, and depending on the types of apps loaded, the actual finished item — the iPhone — powers into action just as you wanted. Regrettably, the comparison doesn't work the same way for us! A phone is easily reset to factory settings and can then be re-programed from scratch. With humans, our brains' plasticity, the factor that allows a vast uptake of information, starts to change during adolescence. It becomes more rigid and absorbs less information. That's why, for example, learning a new language later in life is so challenging. So as a society we spend a considerable amount of time (if not all of it) preparing and programming the next generation to ready themselves for having the best chance of making it in the machine — our commodity-driven economy.

We do this because, in today's world, society pushes us to lead with the mind, which is very dangerous as it can lead us astray by things that are incongruent to heart and body. If you're riding your dragon with the mind-head leading, you're probably suffering from many of the ills that plague our modern-day lives.

When we neglect our body and heart and overuse the mind, there will be many pitfalls on our journey. In reality, the mind, body and heart are inextricably connected, and one cannot exist in a healthy state without the other. In a healthy state, we utilize the energy of each one equally.

If you're relying on your mind way more than your body and heart, it will show in your attitude and quality of life. Let's focus on life quality. Even a century ago, adults and kids died from contagious diseases and infections that turned septic because medical treatment was very basic, and the pharmaceuticals we know today didn't exist. Today, the leading causes of death in the Western World (pre-COVID-19) are lifestyle diseases: an unhealthy diet of fast and processed foods, lack of exercise, stress, anxiety and excessive drug or alcohol use. These daily unhealthy choices lead to high blood pressure, stroke, heart disease and organ failure.

Why do we do it? Partly because the endless consumer marketing machine churns out messages selling us unhealthy food products. Also, people have become hooked on the Internet, so they prefer to spend their time in front of their TV or computer. The kicker, however, is stress and anxiety. They're caused by overworking to either accumulate wealth, or slaving away just to meet basic life necessities whilst enriching someone else. Negative emotions like envy, jealousy, resentment and anger are also common stress and anxiety triggers in our world now. Another very real cause of anxiety and depression is loneliness. Many people are lonely in an overcrowded society. That's simply because we've lost our ability to make genuine heartfelt connections. We focus instead on comparing and judging ourselves and one another.

Then, way too many people choose to ignore their body's pleas for attention, love and care either because they don't recognize them or they don't know how to act on them. If they do decide to change their lifestyle, it often comes from the mind and not the heart. The effort is superficial and lacks self-love. That's why, despite genuine intentions, most people fail at making long-term healthy lifestyle changes. It's a rational, calculated decision measured in units and not goals wrapped in emotions. Ignoring our body can result in lifestyle diseases, including mental health illnesses.

And just as we can't find self-love when we're leading with the mind, we also lack compassion when ⊙ we ignore the heart. That's why we compete with each other and judge instead of extending a hand of kindness. The flip side is that is when we judge others, we also judge ourselves through comparison. Lack of compassion has led to so many living in loneliness, even when surrounded by "friends" because we either choose to hang out with the "in-crowd" or, as a result of rejection because we don't "fit in". Fake permeates every aspect of modern-day life! From living on credit to keeping up with who we "should" be, to working ourselves to death to accumulate wealth, and gathering loads of social media "friends" that we never bond with and don't really care about.

So where do we go from here? Although the dragon analogy made for a neat dramatic entrance to the chapter, it isn't actually the best comparison to help us on our journey.

The same can be said for the heart, and in the following chapter, you can see that the body is just as complex and interconnected.

The three parts — mind, body and heart — form a complex mini-ecosystem which is highly interdependent, interconnected and totally unique in composition from person to person. A bit like a tree!

You can plant two seeds next to each other in the soil and, over the years, two very different trees will sprout and grow from them. As in any forest, every tree looks different yet connects very similarly to its environment.

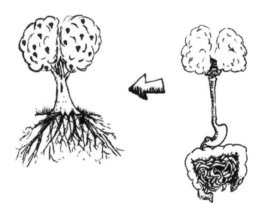

You are that tree! The canopy, like your mind in your brain, decides the direction of growth and seeks energy; the roots are like your guts, ensuring that adequate amounts of good food and water are absorbed as well as being deeply rooted in your overall wellbeing; the fruit is your heart and soul.

No tree can survive without roots and a canopy because both sustain its life. And without bearing fruit, the tree will be the last of its kind because without seeds there won't be any future generations. Trees are also specialized to interact particularly with the ecosystem surrounding them. A tree as a whole supports the survival of many other species as it gladly offers refuge to animals, insects and reptiles, and shares its leaves, fruit and nectar. They also enrich the soil, absorb carbon dioxide and communicate and share nutrients via their roots. Research has also shown that trees release pheromones and slow pulsing electrical signals to warn their neighbors of danger, such as browsing animals or parasitic insects. Once a signal gets picked up, all trees in the area go into defense mode, releasing tannins to make their leaves taste bitter, or scents to attract predatory insects that feed off the parasites. Trees enhance their entire environment.

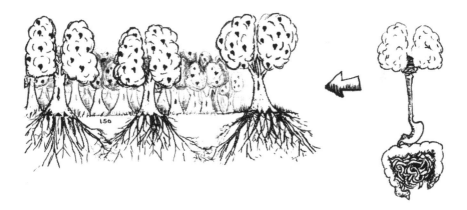

They are very adaptable, enormously complicated, highly perceptive and profoundly intelligent. Each tree is a complete "body" within itself, but also intricately connected with its surroundings. Although a single tree could survive on its own in a grassy area, no tree can truly flourish where there is no other plant life. Trees are interconnected with their environment through equal and mutual give and take to ensure survival. So no, they're not just a big lump of wood.

Imagine if society had been training men to act as trees do!

How Leading With The Mind Impacts Men

Do you know that more men are inclined to die by suicide; or that alcoholism and drug abuse affects men more than women? The root cause of the tragic statistics across nations is our patriarchal upbringing. Men are strong; boys don't cry; are you a man or a mouse? From birth, boys get conditioned to suppress their emotions and focus instead on their strength. Gentle natured boys are quickly bullied and labeled at school by kids and teachers alike. Boys who don't like tough, competitive outdoor activities also get called out and humiliated. And it doesn't stop when they transition into young men and adulthood — the more macho, the better; the more masculine, the more popular.

Countless studies have proven that while the male of our species might be physically stronger than the female, boys display the same levels of caring, nurturing and kindness as girls in early childhood. Despite this, parents and society continue to condition the genders to change their instinctive behaviors. The result? The alpha male who goes through life proving his manliness because that's what he's been hardened to do. Unfortunately, countless men can't keep up with the internal and external pressure, so they either overuse alcohol, take drugs to numb their pain or resort to physical violence. The prisons systems are filled and suicide rates are on the rise.

All of this pain and loss can be avoided if we allow kids to develop according to their own personality by connecting to their own unique calling of mind, body and heart. And talk about it, celebrate it and live it.

There are three responsibilities for those of us whose brain plasticity has already set in leaving us no opportunity to start deep re-wiring in the now:

1. Become aware and reflective! Make a habit of seeing how your three systems are doing –monitor it weekly.
2. Ensure that the people around you, especially the next generation, do it frequently as this forms part of our own increasing self-awareness.
3. Breathe! And breathe with intent....

Since I don't know you personally or your circumstances, there's little value in trying to prescribe ideas that will really motivate you. What I'm showing you is that you can develop more awareness by balancing the mind, body and heart especially through creating rituals. At the end of the book, I'll share some thoughts, exercises and a recording that you can use to shape rituals to suit your own needs.

I do want to mention one thing though that really blew my mind when I spent time with the shaman in Lapland – it was the power of breathing! Or more precisely, drawing air in and releasing it, with or without sound, with full intention and caring attention!

Meditation is still a problematic routine to bring into my daily life despite having tried it for years. There is, of course, yoga. But with my middle age patriarchal ego and dad-bod, the thought of possibly doing yoga seems more like a demeaning encounter to my current existence than a helpful one. Breathing, however, really blew my mind. When I spent time with the shaman, it was the power of breathing and different types of breathing that literally took my breath away!

My research confirmed it: breathing, especially from the diaphragm and belly, is a phenomenal technique not only to connect mind, body and heart, but it also helps shift the internal energy systems from one state to another. Not only does it make the brain more alert, but it can also control the heart rate. Breathing is one of the only main prime bodily functions that isn't controlled by the subconscious. Funnily enough, it's one of the few functions that can be brought to the awareness and into the conscious mind, but once conscious attention stops, it slips back to spontaneous unawareness. It's as though evolution ingeniously knew all along that breathing is super important and a powerful tool to help us maintain balance. I genuinely think that everybody should gift their family and make time for shared breathing practices!

At the end of this book, I'll give you two exercises and some big picture ideas that could form part of daily and weekly practices for yourself and your family. I'll also list the names of breathing experts to help you find breathing routines that suit you best.

Besides breathing, the shaman and I spent a lot of time on all fours in the forest smelling different mosses and chanting to mushrooms – I kid you not! After repeated moss-inhales, the shaman explained that the mushrooms and mosses are the gateways to the forest. I couldn't help thinking that if bankers around the world would stop snorting cocaine and come to the woods to inhale a bit of fresh moss instead, the planet would be in a very different state. After days on the forest floor, an entire universe opened itself to me. As a kid in Africa, I'd already spent a lot of time on all fours with animals and exploring the insect universe, but there was something different and more magical about it this time around. The more time I spent on the floor, the larger it seemed to become. It was almost as if an entire fantasy world opened up within that forest of moss! I was surrounded by towering mushrooms, rows and rows of mini flowers and lakes of berries all teaming with life. And in between were massive, ancient trees – their roots forming mysterious swirling patterns on the ground and their knotted trunks reaching up towards the sky.

It was at this stage that the shaman started revealing his wisdom. He said that today's society focuses on macro things in life. Our careers, the economy, finding the best restaurants, buying the best clothing, going on holidays, choosing with whom to socialize and where to be seen to get the most recognition on social media. He pointed out wisely that there is as much beauty in the micro aspects of our world and, in truth, the micro is actually reflected in the macro. Even when people go for a walk in the park, they focus on the big forest canopy, again enjoying the macro. It's a real shame because sitting down in the forest and taking in every aspect of a small area can be just as enjoyable.

For the shaman, the micro gives him so much more information. When he wanders the forests of Sweden, he doesn't look at the big fauna and flora to assess the health of the forest. He looks at the smaller world and gets a much quicker sense of how the forest is doing, how close he is to water, what minerals are in the ground and which animals are present in the environment.

Why am I telling you this? Because I want you to sit with your tree of life and only your tree. I want you to really learn how your tree behaves. Knowing how your mind, body and heart function is vital, and there's no real point in tackling any of the macro stuff in your awakening process until you feel truly at one within your microcosm.

And if you are male, I want you to go the extra mile exploring your heart, soul and spirit when sitting in your microcosm. As I said earlier, it's an area of the Self in which many men are specifically stunted because it wasn't nurtured. Reawakening to that aspect of your being is the most important thing you can do to realize your own possibilities and in so doing, allow others to do the same.

It's crucial for our mind to be aligned with our soul and spirit so that we can make decisions that feel right. Living with awareness is to allow actions to be guided by the universal source of wisdom and knowledge that creates and motivates everything in the natural world.

We're born to experience life, to experience joy, to fulfill our desires and contribute to our environment in ways that align with our soul's purpose. None of us is meant to be the same as anyone else; that's why we come into this world with a uniqueness that's our own. Through the wisdom of self-reflection and self-knowledge, we can discover the exceptional gifts that we're meant to share with the world.

When we achieve the connection of mind, body and heart, we are in healthy alignment and able to live our lives with real joy.

This is where, as "Boach", I've been doing some of my best work in bars around the world. Men mostly know that they're hurting, or feel stuck – whether in their career, with their self-image and, for those who are more attuned, in their relationships, be it professional, personal or with their partners. A lot, if not all of these conversations come back to lack of knowledge of the Self and therefore making bad decisions due to lack of insight.

The heart is the core of our being. It defines purpose, enlightenment and connection to the universal intelligence or the wisdom of nature. The truth is that we can never experience happiness by suppressing our heart. The mind needs to feed the heart and vice versa. Without that healthy and continuous exchange, life doesn't exist.

By reconnecting with our inner guidance system and raising our consciousness however, our mind can nourish the heart, and we can attain profound peace and inner bliss. Only once the heart can re-establish a connection with the Self and is given equal importance in our inner guidance can we gain true happiness in our own life. That's when we can finally start looking outside of ourselves to create deep-rooted and value-driven systemic change starting within our communities.

Make your heart great again!

Ok jokes aside – let's get to the exercises.

Exercises: Practical Ways To Finding Balance Between The Mind, Body And Heart

Here are some practical exercises that can help you regain balance:

1. **Connecting everything through breathing**

   It's no secret that a meditation session can help center you, allowing you to regain connection with yourself. The body is our connection to all and everything that's going on around and within us. If we want to maintain a good connection with our soul, meditative breathing renews and reinvigorates the connection. Meditation is about breathing, and breathing is about connection.

When it comes to meditation, there are literally millions of experts and articles online giving instructions and advice. It's important to find the best way that works for you. Being a bit of a science head and having learnt about the power of breathing I really latched onto Andrew Huberman PhD, American neuroscientist and tenured professor in the Department of Neurobiology at the Stanford University School of Medicine. ● **'Breathwork, Good Mental Health, & Tools For The Brain With Andrew Huberman'**

2. End of week visualization

Visualize your tree and then in your mind's eye reflect on, and summarize what happened throughout the week, or even just a specific day. Was it stormy, dry or nourishing? Did you bear fruit, or was it more like the forceful flowering of spring? Celebrate the wins, accept the losses and also look at what you can do to rebalance the environment for your tree for the following week.

3. Focusing on the Mind

Finding balance is like a puzzle. You're not really done until every single piece is exactly where it's meant to be. But at the same time, you know that your puzzle has no borders and as you have one area together, the other side has started to disintegrate. Knowing that you can't have all the pieces in one place is about building an awareness of how complete your puzzle is at any given time. Ensure that you're stepping into full pilot, or third-eye mode. Once you can objectively see as much as possible about the condition of your state of mind, then you can make decisions around how you want to use it. There's an old saying that one should only look at one's reflection when the water is still. I know you might be wondering why we're paying attention to the canopy the mind again! Simply because the chances are that your mind is in such an overly powerful state at the moment that it actually needs some extra care and attention to bring it off its high horse so that the other elements have a chance to come out and play:

- *Purify your Mind*

It's crucial to understand that your mind is a vital part of the mind, body, and heart ecosystem. This means that every message sent from your body to your heart has to pass through the mind for explanation. Thus, the mind serves as a crucial instrument between the body and the heart. Therefore, you need to ensure that your mind is free from any forms of illusion that you might be living with. Make no mistake — mastering your mind is a very tough challenge! Your mind is, however, a vital channel and must be treated as such. To be fully functional and aware, it has to be clean and clear. This is one major step towards finding a balance in its entirety.

- *Quieting your Mind*

As you now know, the mind serves as a channel between the heart and the body. However, just like any other conduit, it will only function properly if it's clear of debris. Often many of our thoughts are habitual, based on illusion, unproductive, unnecessary or scattered. Only when our mind is quiet can we sense the subtle communications between the body, mind, and heart.

That's why you need to quieten your mind.

Meditation is perhaps the best-recognized and most effective practice for calming the mind and shifting our focus to *'here and now'*. The goal of meditation is to help you relax and find your inner peace and silence by clearing your mind of thoughts and focusing instead on an object, mantra or breathing. By focusing your mind away from thoughts, you create an inner calm that helps achieve the alignment of mind, body, and heart.

Alternatively, you can also take up journaling as a method of cleansing your mind. It's a great way to clear your mind of all those uninvited thoughts and clutter. When you put your thoughts down on paper, they crystalize into written words that have shape and form. Being able to see them in a tangible format lets them lose any power they have over you. The expression also brings release and frees bottled up emotions. If you want, you can unceremoniously burn your notes to let those thoughts go.

Activities That Reach Across All Areas Of The Tree of life

(But have more focus on heart and body)

There are plenty of activities that can help you find yourself and strike a balance between your body, mind and heart. Here are just a few :

- **Watch what and how you eat:** it sounds funny right? I knew you'd say that! The truth is that today, few understand how great an effect the food we consume has on our body as well as our mind. Eating healthy, nutrient-dense foods will definitely help you to feel more energized and able to tackle your day's problems head-on without feeling you need to reach for that second (or third) cup of coffee. Research shows that there is a connection between eating fast food (junk) and chronic depression. Consider this the next time you're tempted to go to a drive-thru. Also, eat mindfully; feel, taste and smell the food. Try removing other stimuli like sound, media, alcohol and even conversation to absorb the sensation of eating mindfully. Another option is to cook a meal that reminds you of a person, your linage or a country you'd like to visit. Since we're in the process of connecting what's been separated, also think of where the food was sourced, what journey each ingredient took to arrive in your kitchen, and possibly how they feel about being on your plate. Try combining the best food in one mouthful, or the worst; what are the effects and sensations? Does anything come to mind? If you're experimental, eat with your eyes closed or hum a song while eating. Although this might all sound incredibly juvenile, the whole concept of these exercises is that you have everything that you need in front of you or within in you to create change. Keep it low budget, low key and playful.

- **Rest because you need it:** sometimes it feels that taking a break is impossible, but it's not! Have you ever tried to meditate and ended up falling asleep? That's a sign of brain exhaustion! Brain activities are measured through brain waves which come in 5 levels:

  Delta: deep sleep and dreaming (non-conscious)

  Theta: being very relaxed and drowsy

  Alpha: mentally and physically relaxed, reflective

  Beta: awake, alert consciously, thinking and excited

  Gamma: heightened perception, learning, problem-solving, high cognitive process

  Unfortunately, thanks to the information highway that we live in today, our brain waves typically only vary between Theta/Delta followed by long periods of exposure to Gamma activities. In our natural state, we should spend most of our day in Alpha and Beta with the occasional spike to Gamma. Regrettably, though, the age of natural Alpha and Beta waves has long been lost and literally needs to be scheduled in again. The big thing we need is to **take a tech break!** A recent study showed that an average

American adult spends about 6 hours on the phone per day. All that scrolling and tweeting causes your eyes to tire and your mind to absorb too much unnecessary information. Mental fog can quickly develop. Sure, you think that every beep might be from work, or a friend, or that special someone. But continually engaging with handheld devices can have a detrimental effect on our overall health and wellbeing.

Occasionally, try to get away from your phone and other digital devices. Try taking a walk without your phone, or going to the toilet without your phone for a change. *(Yes, I'm talking to you!)* Not only does it affect our productivity, but it also sets us up for more internal struggles. Constantly scrolling on apps like Instagram, where everyone seems to be living their dream only dampens our self-esteem and makes us tap into comparison mode. Too much unfavorable comparison can cause envy, which in turn can bring on depression and self-hate. If this is you, then it's time to disconnect for a bit in the name of self-love.

- **Read a book:** yes, an actual book with pages that you can touch and smell. Engage your mind and activate your imagination as you flip through the pages of any book you choose. *(Although a book with a more spiritual leaning would be a great choice!)*

- **Walk:** I'm not talking about a walk the park walk – I mean walk more in general and allow time between appointments so you can walk instead of ride. Repetitive movement is innately built into the brain and can be incredibly soothing. When we walk we can quickly access our deep-rooted autopilot, relax and take a breather. Remember, human beings were built to hunt and gather… something that might be odd to do on your local high street, but physically buying and carrying things home is more important to your mind, body and heart than you'd think. Buy local to support the local economy; get out and explore and support businesses on your doorstep.

- **Visit a sacred place:** nothing mystical, don't worry. But I find that hallowed spaces such as churches, temples, or other holy places are great spots for reflection and connecting with something larger than your brain and thoughts. These places have been built with clear intent, and we can immediately tune into their purpose, even as we approach them. For me, nature is my church, so I find places within nature or even constructs around nature, be it dams, bridges, wind farms, etc. they all have the same impact for me.

- **Build connections:** Seek emotional connections. We'll discuss our social relationships in an upcoming chapter called 'My Forest'. The connection I'm talking about here is the kind you can do without another person being present. It can be you shifting your awareness to your left foot, or looking at one of your hands as you've never done before (if this feels weird try asking yourself a question like, "If my hand would have a name what would it be and do my hands have a nickname for each other?"). Explore your relationship with things that you surround yourself with — your fridge, the chair you're sitting on, which door is your favorite in the house, do you like your house plants or is there a specific area of the home you really enjoy at a particular time of day? Becoming consciously aware of the things you surround yourself with is super important in building a deeply-rooted, connected life and you do it with all your senses and the mind, body and soul. That's how you bring your microcosm to life!

- **Don't stop learning:** something that might seem obvious, I know. But many people actually perceive their daily scrolling information dump as learning because there's so much information available. Surly that translates into learning? Probably not! This kind of learning is something where you're the pilot. It's driven by an emotional satisfaction that doesn't need input from any external source. The process of learning doesn't need to have an end result in mind and, of course, must be done without any device for the obvious reasons. Now, I am not a technophobe when it comes to devices. I believe that a lot of good can come from them when used with positive intent. But for the benefit of the mind, body and heart connection it's good when devices are turned off once in a while.

- **Open up to your heart's desires:** do what you love! Set aside time each day to do what makes you happy. Many of us work so much that we forget how great it feels to paint, dance, make music, write, garden, or swim. Whatever you do, make sure that it always fuels your passions. Do it for the fun of it and not because you'll gain recognition. Don't run to lose weight, run because you enjoy it! At work endeavor to enjoy the things you like about your work even more!

- **Laugh more:** you know what they say — laughter is the best medicine! And yes it's proven that you can fake it until you make it with laughter so go, go, GO! Singing happy birthday every day to myself in front of the mirror always gets me going!

- **Explore:** many people who are in full autopilot have totally stopped exploring. This doesn't have to involve your entire savings! I am talking about having a hot/cold bath, walking barefoot more often, brushing your teeth with your non-dominant hand, shouting out the name of someone you love or hate and seeing how you react, dancing by yourself, smiling at a stranger. Release your inner child and discover the magical world called life. Begin with simple things, for example, like sucking on an ice cube and maybe before you know it, you're sucking on different frozen fruits to experiment every day.

- **Create a gratitude list:** this is a good one! A gratitude list is a list of things you're grateful for. Before you say **"well, I don't have anything to be grateful for…"** consider that being alive is something to be grateful for. Start with small things and work your way up. Be grateful for your family, friends, pets, food, shelter, health, or the beauty of nature and think about which of the three mind, body and heart elements it truly serves.

How to achieve that mind-body-heart balance? Breathing, meditation and a lot of play. You will still always have a preference towards one or the three, but it doesn't mean it should get the lion's share of your attention; it works exactly the other way around.

This is something that's very important, and kids are inclined to do it more naturally. So if you can live it, they'll follow it. Many of these will reappear when we explore our daily routines and rituals at the tail end of this adventure.

Remember, the world you move in is pivotal for your happiness; speak openly about how everything is interconnected. Connect to linage through food. Connect through food to the seasons.

How To Be Present In Your Body Without Having To Join Yoga Classes (Right Away!)

Here's a summary of things you can do straight after reading this chapter to get going!

- Enjoy a hot or cold bath

- Walk barefoot more at home

- Call a loved one

- Listen to music, dance and sing

- Get crafty, work with materials

- Cook, eat food you love (do it barefooted!)

- Live/think from the heart

- Do things blindfolded with earplugs

- Cry or allow tears to well up

- Go to the toilet without a phone

- Practice deep breathing

- Brush your teeth with you non-dominant hand

- Experience temperature changes (stick your hand in the freezer or cold water)

- Eat without a phone and experience your food whilst focusing on one specific sense

- Laugh out loud — even if it's fake ("faking it until you make it" does work on this occasion)

Just think of ways that enable you to be more physically active in the places you often frequent. I usually remove my shoes during phones calls at work to balance the moment.

Have fun with it! Play!

Generally in life we end up executing too much and don't play enough whilst doing so.

CHAPTER

3

YOUR TRUE NORTH

A h, that fridge moment... yes you know it!

Its post-dinner, but a couple of hours before bedtime. You're meandering through the house or detouring between the toilet and the TV, and you include a trip past the fridge in your travels.

You're not sure why you're there, but you find yourself standing in front of the fridge although you know 100% that there's no need to be there. And before you know it you've opened the door, and your eyes start searching for tonight's needless indulgence.

This is the exact moment when your values come into their own! Tune in to what I call the 'Me FM' radio station, and you'll hear a fascinating talk show between me, myself and I.

"I shouldn't eat anything because I'm already overweight..., "NEVER snack after dinner!" (your mother's voice suddenly echoes through your mind...), maybe just a slice of that salami but I'm not really hungry, and that's a total waste; who bought light mayo, I hate it..., who drank the last beer didn't they think of me..., oh it's a shame that needs heating up..., I should really be looking at the fruit bowl... (sigh)... I wonder why the vegetables get their own area, isn't that food segregation!?..., maybe I should just see the vegetable section as the VIP area, and I'll find them slightly more intriguing ... etc. etc. etc."

Sound familiar? I hope so otherwise I just publicly exposed my own unique inner chatter...

You see our little autopilot has certain boundaries set that we have to abide by to help keep us on track and aligned with our central control system. The wrongs and rights of your universe are called values, your own North Star that you subconsciously navigate by.

Humans face an endless rollercoaster of decision making throughout their lives. Whether big or small, we're making decisions every single second. Like right now I'm currently deciding to keep writing instead of standing in front of the fridge... again!

Although there are a lot of factors we consider before making decisions, the most defining of them are our values. Imagine it as a lightning-fast rollercoaster that the subconscious speeds its decision-making process through without really checking in with the conscious mind. Your core values deeply define you as a person. Why?

a) Every subconscious micro decision taken changes the course of your life.

b) Other people and your environment are impacted by the action you choose and the vibration you give off.

It also provides insight into the kind of person you are or could be, as well as what you want or don't want to do. Often, it's the reason behind our actions and inactions. We see it in the smallest things. For example I think it's courteous to smile back at someone, or, if not funny at least smile at terrible joke, but we all know those who don't. Smiling and humor, in general, aren't set very high on the value system of some people. Values and their ranking are often the cause for culture clashes and things getting lost in translation. Considering I'm half Danish, half German and grew up in countries across the globe, I could write a book about how much we can get lost in the cultural value systems of foreign lands. Often stereotypes of countries and their people are very deeply entrenched in their value system and deliver a rich playing field for many comedians. For those of you who might be struggling with the concept try answering these questions:

Would you rather go to an opening party of the German consulate or the British consulate? Your answer tells you a lot about where your value systems lie. Germans are renowned for investing very little in small talk, make a point of excelling at whatever they are doing and reiterate that they have a leg up on the rest of the world when it comes to engineering, economics and any form of system-based thinking. Whilst at the British opening party the conversation would never really go beyond the complexities of the recent weather front and the contents of todays buffet... and if anybody would dare to venture beyond precipitation talks, it would only be to reinforce the opinion held by many, as giving a truly authentic opinion would be deemed equivocal to streaking through the consulate. Take your pick — it's a conundrum that my British wife and I frequently have!

Often it's when our own personal values are at odds with that of our own nation that we become painfully aware of it.

Anyway, I'm jumping the gun!

If you want to wake up, you have to know what you live by and what values are inscribed in your own personal coat of arms. You have to know what you stand for now before you can attempt to find your more authentic values.

What are your values? Have you ever taken the time to sit down and analyze what your personal value system is? More importantly, have you checked them to see if your external values, which you display to the world, actually match the values of your heart?

Let's first understand values before we get into our self-analysis. All of our attitudes and actions are driven by what we view as important. In other words, what we think is desirable, acceptable, worthwhile or will get us what we want. They give a sense of purpose and meaning to what we do and how we behave and allow us to persevere through times of adversity as well.

And that's what makes values so innately human. They come with a here and now aspect but also a long-term coordinate for guidance that keeps us on track — our track. That's why it's so important to weave your goals with values, otherwise reaching them will be much harder and if reached, they won't be as fulfilling.

When I did an internal check of my values, I was really shocked! I realized that things that I thought were important to me sometimes didn't deliver on their promise. Worse still, I discovered that many of my own inherent values, although present, were actually being sidelined. The level of self-sabotage really threw me.

Mid-way through life, a lot of people get confronted with the notorious midlife crisis, which can turn into outrageous acts of trying to break free from a life built on values that don't really serve you. Which comes as no surprise living in a society that values quantity above quality.

So before you buy yourself a fast car and run off with a hotty at work or, as in my case, run off and live with a shaman in the woods of Lapland, please keep on reading!

While I was trying to figure out these strange values I believed I had to abide by, the picture gradually began to take shape. Many of our set values are often driven by fear and get instilled by people and institutions when we're still very young. We have no awareness or say as to whether we want or agree with them. But because young minds are so open to learning and also vulnerable, we absorb what we're told and accept it as truth. The core of our personal value system is set before we even know we have one!

Being a parent myself, I see how quickly it happens. In the olden days the saying went "It takes a village to raise a kid", but in our modern society, nuclear families do the job alone. And many kids are raised in single-parent households — a trend that's sharply on the rise. On average, today's parents are tired creatures, with little energy left to fight on all the fronts that kids like to push, and should push, since it's part of growing up and learning. So what does that tired parent do? They project blame onto the education system, unhealthy food or excessive screen time. The confrontations are often littered with very divisive language that prompts a fight or flight response. Don't do that because you'll regret it later! The message and its delivery are harsh and set the tone of what should and shouldn't be done.

Both our conscious and subconscious, or Me FM radio station, is riddled with these conditioned values. We frequently access them to evaluate the present through historical events and make decisions in the moment about how we'll respond or what we'll do. Although our point of reference is historic and doesn't apply to current events, we're swayed continuously by what our historically programmed mind tells us.

Eckhart Tolle expects us to be in the now always in order to find joy. I'm a bit more relaxed about it because our biology and society want us to think about time as a continuous spectrum so we should do both. To be living life to the fullest on a spectrum, you must be 100% sure what your values are and if they are true to the Self. It's also crucial that when you're acting on something, you're mindful of the values you're using to make decisions. Understanding our actual values is essential because if our environment, such as our job or intimate relationship, conflicts with our core values, we'll ultimately suffer from burnout or become ill.

We Are Driven By Fear And, Often, So Are Our Values

Current studies of contemporary tribal culture that are reminiscent of our early ancestors show that fear tends to dominate modern life much more than it used to. Although basic survival was always in the forefront of our early ancestors' minds, and they found themselves in perilous situations from time to time, they were more proactive and satisfied with their lives than we are today.

Let's understand why. Life was lived by the hours of sunlight and moonlight as well as the seasons. Winters were a tough time, but they knew that and prepared upfront by drying crops and preserving meat and edible plants during autumn. In other words, they knew that there were difficult times ahead and prepared as best they could. There was also a level of acceptance about what was to come. Resources were shared among the community, and no one was excluded. A successful hunt benefitted everyone. Gratitude and thanks were given to gods and the animal that sacrificed its life for the survival of people. Every part of the animal got utilized in one way or another; no part went to waste. This was done in a combination of respect for the animal and peoples' survival.

Spring and summer was a time of jubilation. Communities repaired the damage done to their dwellings by winter storms and fishermen patched up their boats and nets, and once again took to the water. Crops were planted and nurtured, and people fed off the bounty of nature. The seasons of abundance were celebrated! Massive communal fires were commonplace, and people shared food and ancient stories of wisdom through storytelling, song and dance. There was little resistance (a major cause of stress) to whatever happened, and in the event of natural disasters, people picked up the pieces and either carried on or moved to another location.

How does that contrast with how we live today?

The first and foremost difference is that we don't consider the natural rhythms like the seasons or daylight and the moon cycle; we live by the time on a clock alone. Food and shelter are no longer an issue for most of the WEIRD tribe, but time is something we never have enough of. We're permanently getting chased by the hours of a clock! We have to be on time, race to meet our responsibilities and plan our lives in 24-hour cycles over 12 months. And then there's money! We either never have enough — living from paycheck to paycheck, or enough is never enough, and we're always trying to accumulate more.

Living as we do today creates far more stress than was experienced by our ancestors, and that has an impact on our values. Survival of the clan or tribe has been replaced with interpersonal competition. We don't want to share, and we don't care. How often have you walked past homeless people without even noticing them or wanting to notice them? And if your conscience taps you on the shoulder to show some kindness, your autopilot retaliates with thoughts along the line of "don't give them money they will just buy drugs with it!"

We're continuously comparing, competing and judging. Either we're looking down on others or feeling inadequate. Envy and jealousy and the ego rule where love and compassion should be! As a society, we've wholly separated ourselves on the grounds of fear that someone might outdo us, look better than we do, want something from us, or could be plotting our downfall.

This type of thinking and behavior affects our value system. Positive values bring out the best in us and extend an optimistic and confident energy to everyone in our environment. Conversely, negative values do the exact opposite. They create a state of fear and resentment in both our external and internal environments. Many people who've gained wealth, fame and all the trappings that come with it live in fear for various reasons. Probably the saddest one is that they often don't form real bonds and connections with people because they don't know who they can trust and who's hanging out with them just to gain something, including people on their own scale of wealth or above.

A few examples of positive values include:

- Be dependent
- Show commitment
- Be efficient
- Be free
- Be generous
- Be honest
- Show integrity
- Be kind
- Be fair
- Be motivated

- Be helpful

- Share

- Be honest

Notice how all of these values create trust, whether in a family, business or community. People who share these values are at peace, knowing that they can rely on each other.

We can have negative values programed into us too, that might have had good intentions, but because of the way they were programmed they deliver a distorted reality.

Consider these examples:

- Don't be: poor, stupid, fat, ugly, weak, unsuccessful, alone... the list is endless

- Question everything

- Mistrust

- Fighting to keep your corner

- Guilty until proven innocent

- Looking for differences

- Looking for the worst-case scenario

- Never lose; always be a winner

... I think you get the point!

Notice how these values create fear. Think about how many people you know who constantly criticize, complain and condemn. Maybe you do that! Being surrounded by negatively framed values is very contagious, and people soon become reactive and behave in the same way. Those who aren't willing to surrender their positive values can find themselves pushed to the outskirts with little support. Being treated that way can lead to isolation and feelings of depression all thanks to the reason of cause and effect and the type of feelings and vibrations you give off.

Does that mean that most people today have only negative values? Not at all! The reality is that people don't want to be seen or treated as an outcast, so they follow the crowd, even if it hurts inside. It takes great courage to stand by and live your positive values day in and day out in a world that emphasizes external achievement (the macro things).

How Values Impact Our Decisions

Although life can only happen in the present moment, we can re-live the past and imagine the future in full 3D because our brains can't tell the difference. Past trauma together with our values (not only our own but also societal, family and intergenerational) have a direct impact on decisions we make in the now, which in turn will impact our future.

YESTERDAY TODAY TOMORROW

HOW THE PAST & FUTURE
INFLUENCE THE NOW

"Now"

IDEAL
COGNITIVE
TIME TRAVEL

You must get to know yourself as you truly are, free of conditioning if you want to live your life to the fullest and not end your days in resentment and bitterness. That also means identifying and evaluating the authenticity of your values. So it's time to get out of your co-pilot seat and take full control of the throttle so that you can reclaim your own values and discard those that are just along for the ride and ruining your life-journey.

Why is this so super important? Because your real core values form your North Star. If your North Star is not 100% in alignment with the Self, you'll never arrive at your true destination or even be on the right journey!

Exercise: How To Find Your Real Core Values

Where do our values reside? As much as they seem part of the mind, there are also values in our body and heart. So this exercise isn't a quick and easy one if you want the best results.

I want you to assume that you don't know anything. Clear your mind of all your old preconceived thoughts. More importantly, keep an open mind. One reason why a lot of people find it hard to follow through with some of these exercises is the presumption that they already have the answer from the start. So they don't see a need to embark on a creative, personal discovery process. That's why you must start by adopting the mindset of a beginner. This will allow you access to inner truths to which your conscious mind is yet unaware. Also, ensure you're doing this on an average day and not a day where you're influenced by stuff around you. It's always best to only look at your reflection when the water is calm(ish)!

As with everything in life, there's the earned way filled with homemade goodness, which will most probably end up being more aligned with your true values, and then there's the fast-food version. Because I am a nice guy and I want to give you, and this book, half a chance of actually making it, I'm going to offer you both. Remember to go with your first thought, the information is invaluable for when you kick start your annual planning with the 'elementalist', so write things down.

a) The wholesome goodness approach   ▣

There are three cycles of questioning to find how your inner purpose informs your decision-making process or emotions. It's designed to distill the situation and then chunk it up to bigger concepts. It can of course happen that a person who's well versed in this, or knows themselves very well, can clear this much faster than within three questions per cycle:

Why did you…
And why did you…
And why did you…

What specifically about that did…
And what specifically about that did…
And what specifically about that did…

And if you had more of that then…
And if you had more of that then…
And if you had more of that then…

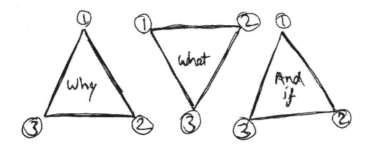

The "why" cycle creates clarity around a situation.

The second cycle drills down on the moment in question to create further clarity.

The last cycle takes the detail and connects it to a bigger thing that's really important to you. #**NB** - Suppressed Values show themselves with negativity framing, so it's imperative to switch from a negative thought pattern to a positive one before you enter the "and if" cycle.

E.g. below **the switch sentence is underlined:**

"I hate my teacher... boss... parent!"

Why do you hate them?

Because they make me do ABC.

And why did you they make you do ABC?

Because otherwise DEF doesn't get done.

And why do you think they say that DEF won't get done?

Because they are controlling.

What specifically about them being controlling doesn't work for you?

It shows that they don't trust me.

And what specifically about **trust is important to you?**

It shows that we're working as a team.

And what specifically about working as a team is important to you?

It gives me a sense of belonging.

And if you had more of belonging in your life then?

I would feel more valued.

And if you felt more valued what would that give you?

Connection.

And if you had more connection?

Love.

In triangulating these three question cycles you find your route to the value, and if the last thing you say is a one-word answer, it could be your absolute core value that often expresses itself as love, freedom or just to be. It's essential to understand the value you have at your core, but the subset of values that you unearth are very significant too, such as connection and value (in the example above). Make sure you pick a situation or opening statement from the spectrum of your life – private, work, hobbies, etc. since there are different values hidden everywhere.

Write them all down and see if you can rank them. Try shuffling them around too; you might find that some suddenly merge or change or even split up. Ideally, we're looking for approximately five values, but it's not a sprint.

Its important to note that you should feel your way through this questioning, as the questioning cycle of 3 isn't of course set in stone... it just works neatly with my triangle theme. ☺

b) *Fast-food option*

For this exercise, here's what I want you to do for me:

You can find tons of value lists online from which you can choose your own, but I don't recommend it simply because we don't select our values — we discover them! And when you start picking them, your mind begins to play tricks on you, telling you that one is better than the other. You can scan a list of values to get a sense of your range of options, though.

From there, you can figure out the ones that truly resonate with you. In his book, ● 'The Confidence Gap', **Dr Russ Harris**, the author of numerous books about **Acceptance and Commitment Therapy (ACT)**, has provided a value list that can help you get started.

While doing this, you might also hear them being said by other voices that come through. Once you hear these voices and you know when they come knocking, write them down like "this is totally something my parents used to tell me" or vice versa. Also, write down the ones you allow yourself because another voice might have a strong opinion against them.

Here's a list of possible values you could consider:

- *Financial security*

- *Compassion*
- *Health/fitness*
- *Nature*
- *Accomplishment*
- *Creativity*
- *Dependability*
- *Loyalty*
- *Beauty*
- *Bravery*
- *Gratitude*
- *Love*
- *Connection*
- *Relationships*
- *Learning*
- *Leadership*
- *Survival*
- *Self-preservation*
- *Security*
- *Adventure*
- *Family*
- *Work*
- *Success*
- *Calm*
- *Freedom*

If you feel inspired add some to this list now!

You can contemplate some of these values listed and use them to create your list. You can list five to ten different values. Over time you might also find that you change your mind. As we take on new challenges and face new situations, we can discover new values or some existing values can become more critical.

Oftentimes, many of our choices are not between right and wrong but between two conflicting values. When this happens, whichever decision we make acts as a pointer to which value we're paying more attention. Also, listen to how you got to the final decision because there's value in that decision-making process as well. If you're not the private type, let your friends and family go through your list too to see how your sensed values and their experience of your values could differ.

Here are some other questions that you can ask yourself to help you move even further into self-discovery:

- What's most important in your life?
- Beyond your basic human needs, what must you have in your life to experience fulfillment:
    - Creative self-expression?
    - A strong level of health and vitality?
    - A sense of excitement and adventure?
    - To be surrounded by beauty?
    - To always be learning?

- What are the personal values you must honor or nurture more?

Also look at people, institutions, artists, scientists, etc. that inspire you and ask yourself what about them motivates/excites you. This also works for superheroes or characters in media and music.

Write your answers down on a new page.

By now, you must've been able to come up with a list of values. It doesn't have to be elaborate. It also doesn't have to be short. Having very few values on your list might not be a pure reflection of your multi-faceted human dynamics. Conversely, too many might just make things complicated. While there is no fixed number of values that you can have, I advise that you stick to anything in the range of five to ten. If, at this point, you already have around 20 to 40 values, however, don't worry.

To get a more concise list, you could try chunking your personal values into related groups. In other words, you combine all of the values you've been able to create using any or all of the processes above to form a master list of personal values. Twenty values aren't actionable! What you can do is to group these values under associated themes.

For instance, values like accountability, responsibility, and timeliness are all related. Learning, growth, and development are interlinked values. Connection, belonging, and intimacy are interrelated too. You can group them together.

Once your grouping is complete, your number should be lower. Now, try highlighting the central theme of each group. Let's say you have a group of values that include trustworthiness, transparency, integrity, sincerity, directness, and truth, select a single word that best exemplifies the group.

For example, integrity might work as a central theme for the values I listed. You can keep the other words in the group in parentheses to give your primary value more context.

CHAPTER

4

THE 6-ELEMENTS

I do enjoy a BBQ!

For my South African friends, I apologize profusely – yes it is a braai!

It's simple and timeless, and I truly love its main aim to be rudimentary, and yet plentiful at the same time.

For me, it's a bit like the Bo-selfie. It's a moment in time where you get the opportunity to escape life's autopilot mode and take stock.

Experiencing the outdoors and the community-building nature of BBQ's are at the heart of what I love about them.

They're educational for kids, and they're fun for all. Roasting marshmallows over the fire, singing and telling stories — it's an experience that connects me with my ancient linage right down to my inner caveman. At the same time, it feels to me that by teaching my kids about the BBQ rituals, I'm setting the scene for generations to come, so in a way, I feel like I'm also connecting to my future. BBQs have, and will continue to be a form of ancestral time travel.

Okay, that might be a touch too far! But in all seriousness, I don't think BBQs get enough credit amongst our main ritualistic meals.

You see, BBQs are a highly ritualized space, a bit like Christmas, where everyone celebrates in their own unique way and then posts pictures on social media, especially if it's their first or last one of the year. Personally, I think how people have a BBQ or what they choose to bring also says a lot about them. When I see only burgers, or vegetable skewers or even fish, I think "you crazy people!" But maybe that's just me.

This isn't, however, a chapter about how to do BBQs. What I actually want to draw your attention to is why this ritualistic outdoor activity has stuck with us over eons. You see, it's within the theatre of BBQs that all that we need gets encapsulated — the 6-elements of life! Because if it was just about eating something that has a BBQ flavor, there are many ways to short cut the arduous set up and clean up that a BBQ brings.

I believe that something happens at a deeper level that might escape today's rushed-off-our-feet society. It is one of the meals that innately brings all the elements together without any effort. Don't see it and why six? Let me walk you through it.

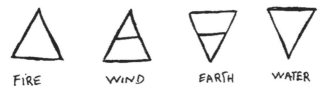

FIRE   WIND   EARTH   WATER

Water, Earth, Wind and Fire:

- **Water** — we all know that BBQs are often well-lubed with alcohol, and it's also the time where elaborate soft drinks are concocted to appease the sober (and kids!).

- **Wind** — an element people would find difficult to compare with a BBQ, but on closer inspection, it's everywhere. It's in the music being played, songs being sung and most notably in the community building conversations and laughter that are at the heart of any BBQ. In actual fact when you think of who you would and wouldn't invite to your BBQ it quite quickly becomes apparent that it's a quite an informative meal; it's a meal that takes a on life of its own, where you might end up burning the food or even worse, the fire doesn't get going. It's a meal where, generally, you invite over the people with whom you can let your guard down and have a good chinwag and laugh about life.

- **Earth** — food! Of course, it's about the food — the explicit representation of the bounty that we get from the earth. It often also forms the pivotal conversation points where everybody compares BBQ traditions and linage notes!

- **Fire** — and then naturally there's the fire! Some people lean heavily into the pre, current and post BBQ fire experience. Others have decided to go down the gas and electric route. At the same time, some swear that it can only be done outdoors to be genuine. Does any of that matter? Not really as long as there is a ritual around it!

So yes, we clearly have the 4-elements, so where do the other 2 come in?

The final 2 elements are the presence of **male** and **female** energies which make up the ultimate spice of a good BBQ! Why bring that in? Well, male and female energies are two of the most vital energies present in our lives! Look at famous philosophy texts, and they concur that everything starts with one before it splits in two — the two opposites quite often referred to as the masculine and the feminine. They are deeply rooted in all cultures, religions, mystic wisdom and philosophies across time, cultures and continents. We've explored the presence of male and female energies since the beginning of time, as well as their interdependence and interconnectivity.

The reason why I'm raising this through the theater of BBQ rituals is that it's quite often in this setting that specific gender roles are reversed, but also played out very obviously, and you know what I am talking about. So it's an excellent scene-setting to create awareness. The other reason is that I know most of you would have jumped ship immediately had I introduced the 6-elements differently because I know that for some (maybe many of you) I've reached the "new age, hippie pain threshold limit" when it comes about talking about the elements. Trust me — I know, because I think I managed to alienate most of the people around me when I couldn't stop talking about anything else but the elements during the endless BBQs we had during COVID-19 lockdown!

So please, hear me out and trust me, it will be worth your time.

The presence of the 6-elements in life and the harmonious balance between them has been the bedrock of many ancient cultures, and I think it's imperative to bring these back as part of our awakening process. I spent a lot of my year deep diving into the belief systems, mythoi and linage around the 4-elements. Ancient teachings included the importance the sun (masculine) and the moon (feminine), and within the matrix of the 6, everything is seen with more clarity — including the Self! It's light-heartedly simple and accessible, but at the same time, it reaches into the depths of global philosophies and building blocks of life itself. It was an eye-watering experience! So, sorry to sneak it in via a BBQ, but it's a great example of how one can understand the deeper reasons as to why something like a BBQ works so well at a fundamental level.

Let's look past the BBQ and see the 6-elements and what they symbolize. After ten years of studying the Jungian archetypes and other forms of psychometric analyses, they're a fantastic filter to utilize for self-exploration and awareness. I started to deploy the 6-elements system with kids and friends. Because of its innate correlation between the symbol and the object with its more in-depth cognitive representation, it meant that people were very quickly engrossed in the exploration rather than trying to understand deep psychological terminology. It also very quickly resulted in kids incorporating it in their BBQ shows and skits for their parents. In a sense, it was as though they naturally understood it but had forgotten the code. What it does is create the perfect micro-universe to hang self-discovery onto because it can be described inter-generationally with little explanation since we already have the foundational meaning of it within us.

I believe we're all born to this planet with a specific recipe for our own secrete sauce… (BBQ sauce)! Yes, precisely the one we are unearthing in this book. So the question is: What are the ingredients to your special sauce when all the ingredients needed in life are water, wind, fire, earth, moon and the sun?

Before we can start mixing ingredients though, I'd like to use this opportunity to introduce them to you… a bit like a Tinder profile of each element!

And yes, it might feel like I'm letting my entire hippy hang out — but bear with me! It's a pleasant journey, and more importantly, it's a massive part of your journey, our journey and possibly for us as a species!

Enjoy your journey into the six corners of the world.

The Sun And Moon

We all have both masculine and feminine energies that move on a spectrum. These energies aren't necessarily something that we're aware of within ourselves. However, boys raised in patriarchal cultures subtly get taught to suppress feminine energy. Denying the energy, however, won't mean that it doesn't still exist within. At the same time, girls get urged to suppress their masculine side as it's deemed inappropriate.

Although, in all, it can be argued that from a societal point of view that an effeminate male is more condemned, shamed and shunned than a tomboy female. Being raised in a system that so deliberately prefers and celebrates one gender above the other has become a very hot topic of discussion, as has the differentiation between male and female genders, biology and sexuality. For the sake of self-discovery, we're mainly focusing on the energies that sit behind the extreme poles of these two opposites. Again everything in life continually moves on a spectrum, but to explain the different aspects one has to separate them to show the points of view. Apart from our own masculine and feminine energies, we're also regularly exposed to them through our environment and external energies that affect us, whether mild or intense.

We must learn to recognize different energies so we can become aware of them. Before we can recognize external energies though, we must understand our own.

This can be incredibly confusing for people like my kids who are riddled with hormones and are navigating this new world of biology, gender and sexuality.

In the olden days, they had a very clear way to express it so that it wasn't confusing. It was the sun for masculine and the moon for feminine.

This requires us to explore our own mind, body and heart to see where on the spectrum of masculine and feminine our energies lie. When we're in touch with our whole being, we can understand ourselves better as we move through the ebb and flow of daily life. The way to do it is to develop an internal radar system that scans your internal environment regularly and, most importantly, in times of stress or when you find that the external world is reacting negatively towards you. Sometimes life happens, and we just go through a tough day, but often, negative responses are because we're emitting bad energy. So get into the habit of checking in on your radar system. Analyze the stats coming out. How does my body feel, what thoughts are going through my mind and how are my emotions?

As you become more in touch with your whole being, including your energy, you'll also become more aware of others on a level much deeper than just the surface. You'll identify energies within people around you and learn how to react to them appropriately by either being more understanding or by taking a tougher stand.

In nature, feminine energy is represented by the moon and water, masculine by the sun and fire. Neither the sun and moon nor water and fire can exist without each other. In a balanced environment, they work in harmony; on their own, they create destruction. That's why it's essential that both men and women acknowledge both energies within the Self and cultivate, nourish and maintain them, as well as become aware of their ebbs and flows.

Here are some examples of energy types:

Sun

- Strong, measured, focused
- Single-task orientated
- Problem solving
- Power centered
- Purpose driven
- Minimizes and undermines things
- Seeks challenge and competition
- Seeks respect and to be needed
- Seeks admiration and acknowledgement

Moon

- Free, flowing, open, joyful

- Multitask orientated

- Emotion driven

- Untamed, destructive

- Nurturing, seeks and gives love

- Seeks open reciprocal communication

- Seeks reassurance and consideration

- Seeks trust, connection and approval

- Recognizes the importance of small things

Both men and women have these, and other energies, on different scales of the spectrum, both negative and positive. Each individual will have a natural or conditioned leaning to different energies. But because energy isn't static, we can work to shift it to improve our lives and that of those around us. Also, as we move through each of our life phases, different energies will naturally come to the fore. If we're in balance and harmony with the Self, this process will be spontaneous and free of resistance. The ability to recognize that we're either experiencing an energy shift or that we're doing things in contrast to our perceived natural state is vital. Once we can see something, we can either accept it or work to change it. Being able to know that we're stuck within one or more energy types helps us move on. Focusing on only a few aspects might empower us in certain areas of life, but it will create blind spots in other areas. A typical example is being overly focused on power and achievement at the expense of emotion and building nurturing relationships. The result for many business tycoons has been that they lose their family along the way and spend their final years lonely and unloved (but living in luxury).

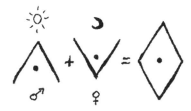

Always keep in mind that we are innately connected to earth and nature through body and heart (female), and to the universal energies through heart and mind (male). In our lifetime, we'll go through many changing seasons within each life phase. When viewed on a spectrum, every life will experience polar opposite situations and fluctuating rhythms, just as in nature. To the un-awakened, these natural sates become confusing, feel unfair and get met with resistance that causes suffering. Once we find awareness, we instinctively understand how to navigate the changing seasons, even if it's painful, because we know that change is necessary for growth.

I urge you to sit down and explore from a mind, body and heart point of view, where on a scale between the sun and moon your energies lie. If you're unsure, give it the classical moon-sun rating. Also, in your mind's eye, observe people around you using this thinking. Sometimes it's easier to start with others than to go within. Also, explore the last conversation you had with someone; did it feel more like a sun or a moon conversation?

I KNOW I sound nuts — but please give it a go.

Think of your current situation right now, what you would like to have more of right now to help you move forward and why? And yes, of course, your "bullshit" autopilot is ringing the alarm bells because this doesn't fit with the program that we're executing. Push through it!

It's pivotal that we all start spending more time in our moon space. There's a lot of talk about having more women in leadership being morally and politically correct. But the bigger picture is that we desperately need to have more feminine energy in leadership (no matter what gender brings it to the table) in order for us to help expedite this current phase of change.

I look to you gentlemen again… if you are still reading that is!

Yes, I am asking you to pull a "mooney" on an emotional level.

WATER

Water plays a central role in many religions and beliefs around the world. It's a source of life and represents birth and rebirth. Cleansing, and by extension, purification qualities, confer a highly symbolic, and even sacred status on water. As a result, it's a key element in ceremonies and religious rites. Rivers, rain, ponds, lakes, glaciers, hailstorms or snow are some of the forms water may take when interpreted and incorporated in cultural and religious ceremonies since it is often perceived as a god, goddess or divinity in religions. Water can represent the border between this world and the other worlds as well. It consequently becomes a symbol of fertility and is regarded as both a giver and taker of life because as much as it gives life when unleashed with the power of nature, floods and tidal waves destroy. When compared to fire, though, water is a nurturing energy.

A quarter of astrological star signs, as well as a quarter of the cards in a Tarot deck used by mystics, represent water. In reality, each of the 4-elements represents one quarter within astrology, the Tarot and compass directions — with water representing "north" as a cardinal point. It's an element steeped in mysticism and magic and often depicted in stories by gods like Poseidon, Medusa and creatures like mermaids and sea nymphs.

Water represents the winter season and is also linked to our circulatory system and blood flow. (The rivers that flow from the heart are rivers of emotion that are particularly important in the symbolism of being rooted or grounded, that's why the capillary rich belly area often gets referred to as "trusting your gut!").

Winter: Although winter paints a picture of lifelessness on the surface, below the ground and deep within, life is flourishing. Way below the surface, the roots of trees continue to draw life-giving water and channel it throughout the tree. For trees, winter is a time of rest and repose to strengthen and bring forth new growth. Darkness dominates the winter months, so the moon is more prominent as trees focus on inner growth. It's also a time when we draw closer to our loved ones through celebration and, take stock of the year that's just passed.

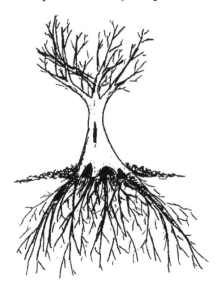

How to recognize water elements in you:

Water elements are driven by a strong need to understand humanity beyond the surface; to peer deeply into the heart of humankind and nurture it to its greatest potential. People dominated by water aren't satisfied with getting to know someone superficially. They want to get to know them on a meaningful and intimate level; to see into the soul. They bring inspiration and are romantics who are driven to meet a potential that's nearly impossible to attain. As lovers of beauty and poetry, they see the world for all it could be and are haunted by the injustices of life. The future is their primary focus, not the present or past. Always championing the oppressed, they're authors of epic stories of good and evil and thought-provoking philosophers.

Information is absorbed through intuition, looking beyond sensory details to find meanings, patterns, and concepts. Rich in compassion and empathy, they consult their emotions and the feelings of others before making a decision.

Because of their extreme sympathy and consideration and their longing to understand others, they can easily step into someone else's shoes and quickly see where they're coming from, even if they disagree with them. Authenticity and depth are essential in their relationships, and they make loyal friends, even when times get rough. They're generous, kind-hearted, and devoted to their friends, kids, and spouses.

Water elements have an intense passion for life and are always seeking to better themselves and others. Quick to see potential in everyone and every situation, they live with a restless longing to meet that potential. When entering into relationships and friendships, they go in wanting to know a person's mistakes, flaws, darkness, and accepting them as they are. Concurrently, they encourage their loved ones to achieve their greatest dreams and highest standards by exposing their light, beauty, and passions.

Extremely perceptive about people, they trust their intuition very strongly when it comes to insights and revelations about people or the future. Often they can sense whether someone is lying or putting on a façade. As a result, they can read things into people and reveal insights that others are totally oblivious of. This ability makes them dedicated in vocations such as teaching, social work, counseling and journalism. Clairvoyance or foretelling future events is not beyond the powerful intuition of the water elements. They notice signs and pathways that could develop based on patterns and veiled meanings that go primarily unnoticed to others. Sometimes their visions of the future are ominous and eerily accurate; a side of them that may take their friends and family members by surprise. Although warm and eager, they often struggle within because of their ability to see things that could lead to adverse outcomes or cognize clues that they'd rather overlook.

Even if they choose not to follow to a specific religion, they're naturally very spiritual. They seldom accept things at face value and are more drawn to connotations and implications behind all things. Patterns, forces, forecasts and meaning are more significant to them than their senses of hearing, sight, smell, taste and touch. The water element is less likely to choose not to believe in a god or spiritual realm since they "can't see it or feel it". Because they trust intuition and insights that are often unseen, the water element has a natural affinity to the spiritual and mystical side of life.

Another positive quality is that they make excellent peacemakers. They hate conflict, yet they can be just the types you need when a dispute arises. Their skill at seeing all perspectives of a situation and finding a link that will connect enemies, allow them to open a doorway to making amends.

Since they crave harmony and unity, they spend a lot of their lives putting out fires, soothing hurts and bringing good will back to those around them. If you're going through a conflict with someone, they can give you great insight into how you can resolve the issues you're facing. Water elements are naturally tactful and empathetic, making them masters at influencing people's attitudes and inspiring them to grow, understand each other, and settle their differences.

You might have felt that this spoke to you in parts or directly; both are totally okay. This is more about how much of this quality you think you have within you. Other people in your life might have popped up in your mind as you read this. If so, excellent! You're becoming aware of elements that you surround yourself with.

For those of you who felt a clear leaning to this description and expect to have a lot of water element within you, I'd like you to go a little deeper.

Let's say the majority of you is water: are you the stream and murmurs quietly in background minding its own business, or are you more like the Victoria Falls, the center of attention that people go out of their way to see? Of course, I'm using extremes to over exemplify that most of us have the capacity to be both, but left to your own devices, which would you tend to be?

Note it down: calm and tranquil or powerfully cascading waters?

WIND

Wind is also referred to as "air" and associated with the cardinal point "east", where the sun rises, bringing change, wisdom and communication from faraway places or worlds. It's in these far-off places that winged beings like fairies often live in fairytales. Usually, they're the keepers of knowledge or creatures you can turn to for advice. These beautiful beings also travel from afar to bring messages of wisdom and learning, or they come from far afield bearing messages about other worlds. They're represented by the likes of white doves or the crows of Nordic traditions, Apollo, Hermes, Pegasus, unicorns, genies or magic carpets.

Wind represents the season of spring and also links to our respiratory system. The respiratory system is often not given the level of attention it deserves (but maybe now with COVID-19 the lungs are getting more attention than ever). It's our respiratory system that enables speech and song and laughter! All things that have been gifted to us through evolution and make us such a unique species. Through the respiratory system, we can vocalize thoughts, dreams and emotions. Like spring, through the spoken word and song, the birth of something new can initiate great things that will enable us to bear fruit later in life. Our respiratory system is also responsible for connecting mind, body and heart. It can express joy and deep sadness and has the power to transition us from one emotion to another, just as spring transitions us from cold to warmth. ● 'Breathe to Heal', Max Strom, TEDxCapeMay

Spring: Warm winds awaken the forest, as blossoms appear everywhere together with new shoots, baby birds, lambs, calves and insects. Spring is a time of action, color bursts, the energy of new life and the promise of the bounty to come. The spring equinox is when the feminine and masculine energies merge and are in total equilibrium.

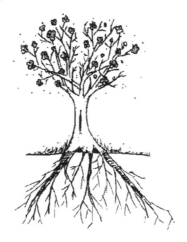

How to recognize air elements in you:

Air is a free spirit who thrives on living boldly and embracing the moment fully. Easy going by nature, air elements possess a strategic intelligence and can see opportunities as they arise. They have a natural talent for knowing how things work; whether it's art, fashion, machinery, or a business deal. Fun loving and optimistic, they're some of the best types to have around in a crisis. Thinking quickly on their feet, they can make the best of any situation, no matter how gloomy it may seem to someone else. Impulse and excitement drive them on, and they love traveling and seeing new sights and experiencing new feelings. Fascinated by the world as it is, they long to go out and explore all that it has to offer. Their optimistic and daring nature means they're always looking to explore more wonders and sounds and tastes and experiences. Naturally playful and creative they live with a strong desire to try new things and boldly take on new adventures.

Air elements absorb information through sensation; what they can see, smell, touch, taste, and hear. They're incredibly aware of their outer environments and how to adapt to them. Easy-going and laid-back, air elements are as spontaneous as the wind. Tight-schedules or strict guidelines make them feel stifled, and they prefer making decisions on the fly and adapting to situations as they arise.

With their intense zest for life, air elements don't spend time grappling over the past or worrying about the future; they know how to make the most of the here and now. Air elements are impulsive, adaptable, courageous and competitive. Because of their fascinating mix of impulsiveness and practicality, they tend to accept the world as it is. Hypothesizing about the many "what if's" in life doesn't interest them. For those who are more focused on the past or future, their flexible and spontaneous aptitude is confounding.

Another hallmark of the air element is that they're hands-on. They love to be moving, working with their hands, and using their bodies. Even though these abilities can occur in all elements, the air element seems to have an innate craving to explore them fully. Many air people are natural athletes or dancers because of their awareness of their environment and how to navigate the physical world proficiently.

One more characteristic of the air element is their ability to take risks and bravely explore options that other types might be afraid to try. To them, life is an exhilarating journey packed with different prospects that shouldn't be missed. They love to take advantage of the moment, no matter how scary it might be or what may happen as a result. This audacity and free-spirited nature makes them compelling and attractive to many other personality types.

The air elements differ in their strengths; some have masterful use of moon energies and others, sun energies. Moon air elements have a fiercely independent set of values and emotions that influence everything they do. Compassionate, kind-heartedness and gentleness are automatic to them. However, they're not easily swayed when it comes to their beliefs and morals and have a firm grasp of their core value system. The origins of their beliefs are internal, shaped by their own thoughts and feelings. It's highly improbable that they'll be influenced by the crowd or their environment when it comes to their core values. Moon air elements often have deep love and compassion for kids, animals and those less fortunate. Inevitably, they'll defend the underdog in situations of bullying or exploitation. This sense of empathy often gets infused into their artwork, performances, or the music they enjoy listening to.

Sun air elements are deeply invested in their outer world, seeking to expand their knowledge and discover details and facts. They want to take things apart to figure out how they work and how they're put together again. Naturally hands-on, they learn through experience and are quick to grasp the innate design and purpose of tools and machinery. Striving to remain logical and objective in all their decisions, they pride themselves on keeping a steady head no matter what circumstances arise. They're excellent at problem solving, troubleshooting, and overcoming challenges as they happen.

You might have felt that this spoke to you in parts or directly; both are totally okay. This is more about how much of this quality you think you have within you. Other people in your life might have popped up in your mind as you read this. If so, excellent! You're becoming aware of elements that you surround yourself with.

For those of you who felt a clear leaning to this description and expect to have a lot of air element within you, I'd like you to go a little deeper.

Let's say the air element dominates you: are you the quiet summer afternoon breeze that gently blows through, are you the "let's get our kites out" kind of wind, or the kind of wind that gets neighborhoods worried or even makes it onto the evening news? Of course, I'm using extremes to over exemplify that most of us have the capacity to be all three, but left to your own devices, which would you tend to be?

Note it down: gentle, gusting or gale-force winds?

FIRE

The power of fire holds a magnetic attraction for us; that's why we like to stand around it at BBQs and stare into the flames. As a cardinal point, fire represents "south". It's a purifying, masculine energy, connected to strong will and drive. Fire both creates and destroys, and symbolizes the virile fertility of the elements.

In many magical traditions, fire is associated with various spirits and elemental beings. For instance, the salamander (your everyday garden lizard) is an elemental entity connected with the power of fire, making it a magical and fascinating creature. Other beings associated with fire include the phoenix (a bird that self-destructs through spontaneous combustion and then gets reborn from its own ashes), and of course, dragons who are known in many cultures as fire-breathing destroyers and the keepers and protectors of ancient wisdom and riches.

Fire is associated with the summer season and linked our nervous system. Compared to the other elements and body systems, this element draws a lot of attention which comes as no surprise since it's the element that has the most masculine energy. Revered over millennia across the world, fire has often been worshipped through gods like Ra, the ancient Egyptian sun god. Evidence tells us that fire and the sun have been a pivotal force from the Iron Age through to the industrial revolution, and both World Wars. In fact, the taming of fire is deemed to one of man's most extraordinary evolutionary steps (clearly told from a patriarchal version of history). So we don't need to give it that much attention here because we already know a lot about it. Truthfully, we've given it so much attention that it's actually the one thing that might kill us since it's at the center of global warming and climate change.

Summer: As the sun moves closer to the earth, a vibrant energy begins to build, strengthening all of nature. Tree twigs sprout and strengthen into new branches, blossoms turn to ripening fruit, baby birds become fledglings, and lambs and calves stand strong bedside their mothers. The forest is burgeoning, robust and in full swing, sustaining an abundance of life and nourishment. At the summer equinox, the full masculine energy of the sun is at its peak. Whilst in winter, people connect to their loved ones, summer is a time to get things done — to build and complete projects. During summer, we're often focused on things rather than emotions.

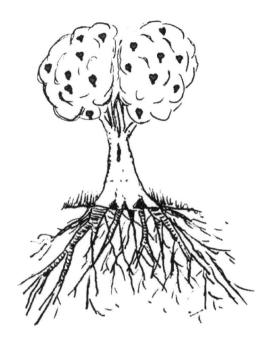

How you can recognize fire elements within you:

Fire is driven by a strong need to understand the complexities of the universe and to explore new theories, concepts, and ideas. Fire elements are logical, abstract and theoretical. Understanding the very truth about everything matters very much to them, as does being objective in all their decisions. Innovative, progressive and frequently ambitious, they tend to be independent. Often they become driven entrepreneurs, deep-thinking scientists, acclaimed inventors, philosophers, and politicians. Their ability to notice patterns and trends is quicker than in many other types, and they can quickly gather insight into the future of organizations, systems, and elaborate plans.

Fire elements absorb information through intuition; looking beyond sensory details to find meanings, patterns, and concepts. Their strong sense of logic and focus makes them objective and truthful in all their interactions and decisions.

Albert Einstein and Stephen Hawking are the epitome of fire elements, who possess(ed) an extreme need to uncover the truths of the universe. Some of the most distinguished thought-leaders in discovering new theories and revelations that have made radical advances in our understanding of science and the universe are fire elements. Fire is a natural learner and teacher, always expanding their mind and looking for new ways to experiment and apply what they've learned.

A quick-thinking, logical mind makes them excellent strategists who can provide insights to educational organizations that sets them apart from their peers. Many university professors have a lot of fire elements.

Excellent at solving problems and understanding systems, they can improve nearly any program, no matter how complex. And it's not only real-world application of their problem-solving abilities that they strive towards; they also learn just for the sake of it to expand their knowledge. Open to learning from anyone who has something useful to teach them, they will, however, ignore anyone (irrespective of their rank or authority) who seems incompetent or unable to discuss things logically.

It's unlikely that they'll accept anything at face value and they can be skeptics. Every decision and belief gets scrutinized and critically analyzed before they allow it into their lives. Endlessly curious, they believe avidly in the complex nature of things. On the one hand, they're skilled debaters, and on the other, they're entirely willing to consider new ways of approaching problems if their challenger is logical and well informed on the subject.

Independent and strong-willed individuals, fire elements will seldom submit to external influences or peer pressure. Their independence is vitally important to them, so to outsiders, they can come across as cold and matter-of-fact. However, fire is often loyal and open-minded when it comes to interacting with new people who are also curious or love learning. Many fire elements have deep emotions and feelings that they'll share with only a select few. Nonetheless, they adamantly refuse to be swayed by these emotions and pride themselves on keeping a level head and remaining objective as much as possible at all times.

You might have felt that this spoke to you in parts or directly; both are totally okay. This is more about how much of this quality you think you have within you. Other people in your life might have popped up in your mind as you read this. If so, excellent! You're becoming aware of elements that you surround yourself with.

For those of you who felt a clear leaning to this description and expect to have a lot of fire element within you, I'd like you to go a little deeper.

Let's say the majority of you is fire: are you the quiet radiator that warms the house on a cold winter's day, the fire that takes center stage at a BBQ, or the dazzling fireworks display at a festival. Of course, I'm using extremes to over exemplify that most of us have the capacity to any of these, but left to your own devices, which would you tend to be?

Note it down: quietly warming, drawing in a crowd with your flames or lighting up the night sky with thundering colors?

EARTH

Earth's cardinal point is "west" where the sun sets; a time to reap the benefits of your daily toil as well as prepare for the night to come. In fairytales, dwarves, trolls, gnomes and other creatures are said to protect the mysterious world of earthly treasures (mines, precious stones, water springs and fertile fields). There's been a popular resurgence of these mystical beings in mainstream media through books, TV series and movies including 'The Hobbit', 'Lord of the Rings', 'Harry Potter', 'World of Trolls' and 'The Smurfs'. Previously people believed that earthly treasures were supervised by various tiny supernatural beings who appeared everywhere in the forests, old tree hives, mountains, mines, marshes, next to domestic fireplaces, in blacksmiths' workshops and shoemakers' shops. They're also especially busy during the autumn working as Father Christmas's helpers, which is how most kids first come to know about them.

Earth connects with autumn and our metabolic system.

The metabolic system is a bit like the circulatory system because it connects the body to the heart via our second brain in the belly; the place where clear emotional thought happens without ego or social programing. It's the authentic you that connects to mother earth. We need to spend much more time there, and the quickest way out of the mind (fire) is via wind (breathing) to get to the belly, earth. Autumn is the season of abundance after the harvest when people used to fatten up to build reserves for the winter months. Even today, we tend to eat more in autumn and winter because our bodies require more fuel to keep us warm. And remember, you are what you eat so metabolism should be honored during this period, all the way through to Christmas.

Autumn: As the sun begins to move away, the days become shorter and the nights are longer. Birds start their migrations, leaves begin to fall, hibernating animals prepare their burrows, and other animals develop their winter coat. It's a highly operational season with limited time to get things done. Everyone is doing their final harvesting before the forest once again settles into a time of restfulness. The seasons are coming full cycle, and at the autumn equinox, the masculine and feminine energies once again merge into total equilibrium.

How you can recognize earth elements within you:

Earth elements are a beacon of stability and loyalty in the swirling chaos of the modern-day world. They're driven by a strong sense of responsibility, dependability, and justice. Hard working and honest, they are people you can truly depend on to keep their word. They long for security and stability in their lives and strive to give these same comforts to others. Dominated by a strong sense of right and wrong, earth elements will defend their beliefs irrespective of any opposition they may face. Upholding law and order and maintaining morality is essential to them. Familiarity and consistency help them feel at home in the world, and they strive to be a stable presence in the lives of their loved ones. Earth elements are to be respected for the dedication and care they provide in practical ways to those around them.

They're acutely aware of their inner body sensations; feelings like hunger, thirst, illness, and pleasure. Preferring to live practically, they're often described as "down-to-earth". For them, the world needs to be understood in a concrete, realistic way, and they strive to be level-headed in everything they do. Organization and structure are their presence. Planning ahead and knowing what to expect makes them feel at ease and they're inclined to make detailed to-do lists for all their projects and deadlines.

Practical tried and tested techniques for solving the problems that come up from day to day is their ideal approach. And although they like to be prepared for the future, they also want to draw lessons from the past. Earth elements have a keen respect for history and love traditional learning methods. Many earth elements need to be in harmony with the past, so they take up traditional hobbies such as woodwork, blacksmithing, soap and candle making or quilting.

With an intense eye for detail, they often have meticulous memories of past events and experiences. Annual celebrations that help them have fun and commemorate family, holidays and pastimes matter to them as is being involved in close-knit families and communities.

Naturally responsible, earth elements believe in fulfilling their obligations and plans to the best of their abilities. Consistency, dependability, sensibility, and thoroughness in all their endeavors are high on the list of their values. Their realistic attitude towards life is based on being grounded, having an eye for detail and learning from past experience.

Earth elements will vary depending on their preference for sun or moon energy. The sun earth element values objective logic and balanced thinking. Before making a decision, they look at all the pros and cons, consider the facts and analyze what makes the most sense. Their approach to logic is realistic and practical, and they use analysis to determine what option will best help them solve problems. Something they see as having no practical application at the moment draws no theoretical logic or debate from them. Selflessness is a core trait, and they want to solve problems within their communities and provide hands-on support to those who need it.

Sun earth elements are excellent at handling logistics. In fact, they have the most robust logistical intelligence of any of the other elements. Where sun earth elements are excellent at organizing systems and programs efficiently, moon earth elements almost seamlessly organize community and social events so that all people feel a sense of coherence and belonging.

Moon earth elements are excellent in nurturing roles because of their hands-on sense of kindness and compassion. If you're sick, they're the ones who will ensure you get a meal, or they'll give gentle guidance and proactive help. To them, the best way to care for someone is through providing practical support. They're inclined to show loyalty to their families and communities through acts of service and generosity. When it comes to making decisions, the moon earth element will try to step into the situation and empathize with the people involved. They need to perceive how their decisions will affect the overall harmony of the group and the emotions and well being of others involved. They love to be part of a community and do what they can to serve others and live life as open-heartedly as possible.

You might have felt that this spoke to you in parts or directly; both are totally okay. This is more about how much of this quality you think you have within you. Other people in your life might have popped up in your mind as you read this. If so, excellent! You're becoming aware of elements that you surround yourself with.

Let's say the earth element dominates you: are you the gentle rolling meadow tucked away in a forest only to be spotted by the occasional wanderer, or the epic Himalaya or Grand Canyon that people travel from far to see, and can't miss even if they tried? Of course, I am using extremes to over exemplify, most of us have the capacity to be both, but if you were left to your own devices, what would you tend to become?

Note it down: calm earth or excitable, spectacular earth?

So What Is My Secrete Sauce?

I hope you've been taking notes. I'd like you to now write down in one sentence that makes sense to you what your magic sauce recipe might look like.

And just like cooking and throwing a BBQ, it's not an exact science. You're just putting it on paper for the first time. And for you more earthy and windy elements, please feel free to use only the words that spoke to you if the concepts are a bit abstract for you.

The sentence could sound something like "I'm a major fire with windy/watery tendencies, my body sits solidly in the sun while heart and mind are represented by sun and moon."

I was totally gob smacked how kids had theirs down even before I tried to explain it further. Clearly, they're less programmed by society and took to the concept like ducks to water.

For the middle-aged reader, handling this information might be not so easy. Please don't worry about it! Maybe it's the first time in your life that you've written down a sentence like this about yourself. You've opened up an awareness that you can start giving more presence to. Later in the book, we'll give it much more attention especially when it comes to your goal setting because being knowledgeable about the 6-elements is the perfect shorthand for creating awareness about your own tree of life as well as the forest you're about to meet. And trust me, if this was your first time — like with all first times in life — there is a lot of practice needed before you become good at it.

You'll also soon find out that your secrete sauce recipe will change depending on who you're with. While each tree in a forest appears to be separate from the rest, the whole forest is deeply connected. During their lifetime, trees endure many seasons, and each one comes with different elements. For us, it's much the same. Although superficially we're individual, we're intricately connected with family and everyone else around us. Trees connect through their root systems, so establish who your roots are connected to and understand what season they bring and what purpose they share in your life and vice versa.

There's no coincidence in the turning of the seasons and the elements that come with it. Each one has its purpose, and everything happens in perfect synchronicity and precise timing. And this all occurs spontaneously on a scale that humankind can hardly imagine. Everything is taken care of in the minutest detail. Just think about it — as hibernating animals need to line their burrows, the forest floor becomes covered in leaves and summer coats are shed by other animals, providing them with ideal burrow insulation. The dead leaves also create a layer of warmth to protect the roots of the trees from cold and frost.

And instinct prompts migrating birds to gather and fly. It's planning on a scale that defies the human mind.

Before We Move On

It goes without saying that making broad brushstroke characterizations about people who, in actual fact, are very unique in their own right goes against what this book actually stands for. This is not a dogmatic system that boxes you up as an element. There's absolutely no prescribed approach to this, and like the directions of a compass, these should just guide your self-discovery. It doesn't dictate the one or the other, like with a compass you never actually reach true south or north; it's just a guide towards a direction. So have fun with it, don't take it as rules set in stone; there are many degrees between the seasons and landscapes and all sit on a spectrum. For example, if you sit between fire and earth, you might come across as an extreme desert environment type of person. That's not to say that it can't get likened to the Okavango Delta in certain seasons or moments of your life. But knowing this will help you, and especially younger generations, speak about their own or other inner worlds.

If you had a real "aha" moment during this chapter and want to become even more scientific about this, please do so. All of the info about the 4-elements is built on research offered here: ● Psychology Junky.

I wanted to finish this chapter off for those of you who really struggle for two reasons. Some might see themselves in everything and feel as though they have all elemental qualities in them. Well, congratulations! You've won the jackpot because you can fit in anywhere and everywhere – a bit like ketchup; you're the type of person who is very fluid, your magic sauce belongs at any BBQ. Then there could be those of you who felt so at home in one particular element that you couldn't even understand or be interested in discovering other areas. You're the type of magic sauce that comes with one specific strength — a bit like chili sauce. It's not for every day, but when you need it, you can't think of anything else. What this means is that you have an absolute superpower that people might already be seeking out because you deliver it so instinctively. Many people who come with these superpowers often come with kryptonite, which regularly reveals itself on the exact opposite side like a pendulum. Which would mean -

- Water- Fire
- Earth-Wind
- Moon-Sun

If you're one of these individuals, seek out balance wherever possible either with people, or action and plans. You're much needed in your community for your superpower, but at the same time, you really need them to protect you from your kryptonite.

There's a third and final type of person who might have stumbled across something: as seasons and the weather, they should be able to come and go, but as you were reflecting on yourself, you realized that you always seem to be stuck in the same season or weather. And you have a real sense that it's impacting the joy and relationships in your life. Please take my advice and start speaking to people about it (also refer to the section on "boundaries" in the Forest chapter.) This could be a sign of something else. Something that doesn't really reflect your secret sauce but rather something that needs to get tackled with different guidance than offered here.

CHAPTER

5

WHO AM I XL – MY FOREST

I hope that men especially have their pencils sharpened for this chapter!

This chapter is the one that gets me most excited because it covers precisely how and where we, the WEIRD tribe, lost the plot and how we can regain it very fast.

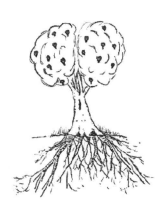

Without throwing you in at the deep end, I want to remind you of your tree of life. The canopy and roots focus more on the inner universe. They do, of course, live and connect with the external world to get info and nourishment, but their main activity is much more "I" focused compared to the third element, the heart. Emotions are a huge part of us and play a significant role in our internal decision making. But compared to the other two parts, the heart is the part of the Self that spends most of its time connecting to the outside world. Consider flowers and the fruit they bring forth; their prime function isn't only the continuation of the species, but also to feed and nourish the world around them. That way, they connect with the ecosystem in a meaningful way.

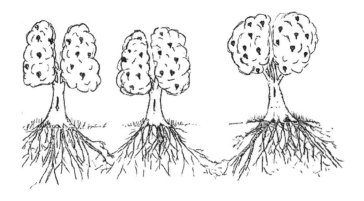

But what really blows my mind (and I do LOVE it when an analogy keeps on delivering), is that although a tree, just like you, is its own microcosm — the fluidity with which it connects to its bigger eco-system of the forest is breathtaking. We all know that a forest is an eco-system, but are you aware of the extent to which trees communicate, trade and even nurture each other? Trees support each other to the point that ailing trees, as well as saplings that would have a tough time surviving on their own, are sent extra nutrition via compacted root/soil collaborations. Think about the impact of deforestation. At the rate we're going, destroying natural forests we could soon reach the tipping point beyond recovery. A place where it will be super hard to turn things around again. Fellow flora and fauna aren't a nice-to-have, but a must-have for the balance of life to remain in equilibrium.

And it's precisely the same for humankind! The "me, myself and I", in actual fact, can't live life without the "you, them and us"! Never underestimate the importance of relationships and connections to us as a species. We already saw this when we first set out with your Mirror, Mirror on the Wall exercise. As Adam Leipzig said: *"An unexamined life is not worth living."*

The poignancy of this is that 60% of his questions, which we looed at in chapter 1, are not about you but the people that around you.

Here's a reminder:

1. Who am I?
2. What do I love to do?
3. Who do I do it for?
4. What do they want or need?
5. How do they change as a result?

Now, when talking about the others, I'm not speaking about the pictures that you posted on social media to harvest likes;

no, I am referring to the people who form part of the very fiber of your being and are an extension of you.

Humans are social primates. More than by any other factor, our experiences and behaviors are affected by the company we keep. Our lives are inescapably linked to other people and our environment. Everything, from our immune system to our genetic makeup, is affected by the microbiome we all share by spending time together. The mirror-neuron effects actually alter our neural networks so that we can find meaningful significance with the people around us. In reality, we're the average of the five people we spend the most time with. Without consciously exploring and improving the quality of our relationships, we're not unlocking their potential.

According to British anthropologist Robin Dunbar, our brain capacity only allows us to have up to 150 intimate relationships. Beyond that number, intimacy and our knowledge of people drops steeply.

That got me thinking: if having a connection to people is so pivotal that it can literally be considered as an extension of our own biological makeup, AND there's a precise number, why don't we as the WEIRD tribe have a better strategy around that? Why don't we teach our kids that you have one mind, one heart, one body, and one people — and they all form **YOU**!

Think about it — these people are our emotional bedrock, our day-to-day support system, so in reality, they're our forest! Society is just a jungle littered with loads of mini-forests, and each one of us is at the center of a forest. So since we're reconnecting with our tree of life, it would be rude not to reconnect with the rest of us, right?

Humans Are Social Creatures

Before we've connected with our body and heart on a deeper level, we might not appreciate how important the people who surround us are to our survival. Through awakening our internal connections, we realize that we're not a solo entity, but part of a thriving ecosystem that has many extensions. However, we can't fully comprehend our ecosystem until we understand how it's formed and how we can manage it.

This is where Dunbar's 150 connections come in. His research found a direct correlation between primate brain size and their social group size. Applying that data to their closest relative, human beings, Dunbar speculates that 150 connections are the most we can handle. If he's right, the WEIRD tribe can comfortably maintain 150 stable relationships. Dunbar explained it informally as "the number of people you would not feel embarrassed about joining uninvited for a drink if you happened to bump into them in a bar." 'Dunbar's number', Wikipedia

As a species, humans are innately social creatures. We need the interaction, companionship and support of others, that's why we value family and also form external bonds. To prove it, think of solitary confinement which has been used as a form of discipline and torture over thousands of years.

Of course, we don't all necessarily have or even want 150 connections. Much depends on our personality, where we live, our career and what type of hobbies and activities we prefer. The next question is – how accurate is this today's world of social media? Via social media, we can have a vast number of acquaintances, but how intimate are these connections and do they form part of our ecosystem? Dunbar claims that his theory is as correct for early hunter-gatherer societies as it is for us today. So we can safely assume that this number includes social media connections as well. When analyzed — office settings, communes, factories, residential campsites, military organizations and even Christmas card lists rarely exceed 150.

Knowing that social interaction is part of our evolution, a fundamental part of our biology, and has a precise finite number, we should really start treating them as a natural and quantifiable extension of our physical being. It's not too dissimilar to our new understanding of how trees communicate danger through pheromones and electrical signals and use their roots to form a vast web of connection which is the absolute bedrock of any forest ecosystem.

You cannot live your best life without knowing who's in your forest. It's here, specifically, that we as a WEIRD tribe have unlearnt our ways. Just think about it — it's mind-boggling! Social connection is part of our natural genetic and physical makeup, which means it should be one of our most significant resources. Best of all, it's free of charge!

So, who are your 150?

For me, this is where my gypsy lifestyle experiences come in very handy. When you've moved countries more than eight times, you truly get a sense of how important people are to your existence and how painful it is when they all disappear overnight. It's like deforestation in one fell swoop! Although traumatic, it comes with the gift of rejuvenation. Once you've started rooting down again in the new place, you start rebuilding your forest. Although it can be draining it also gives you "a mirror, mirror on the wall" moment when you can actually ask yourself "who do I need on my next leg of the journey?" And this is where I get very excited because "what do I need" is also a way of asking "what do I need to give?" But that's for later chapters.

Relocating so often taught me how to regrow my forest frequently. Over time you become an expert in setting up camp fast, but also very good at sowing and nurturing new seeds and encouraging growth.

The Clan, The Hoard And The Muse

I like to split the 150 connections into three groups: *the clan, the hoard, and the muse.*

The Clan

These people are your linage: blood relatives as well as old school, university friends. Generally, the people that surrounded you whilst your brain placidity was craving and absorbing every life experience. That's why these relationships are so deeply rooted in your emotional landscape. The shared experiences you had form part of your brain structure and were woven into the fiber of your being. Obviously, these early connections will include people who've passed away, but if you shared a deeply intimate relationship, you could still have an inner dialog with them.

The clan members are very close to you and will stay with you until the day you die.

The Hoard

This is the second group. It's made up of your transactional tribe. These are the people that you interact with every week to make life happen in the here and now. The communication and interactions that occur can be in your professional or private capacity.

These can be colleagues, bosses, neighbors, parents of your kids' friends, teachers as well as your hairdresser, butcher, local bartender or the one postman that you've clicked with and are happy that their round and your lives have crossed paths. The hoard is the part of the tribe where a lot of transition takes place. The boundaries are porous, and people come and go over the years. Regardless, they're still vital to managing the daily wear and tear of everyday life, particularly when it comes to working on your connection levels in the here and now.

The Muse

The third group is unrestricted, and there's less attachment. These are the people you seek out for non-essential activities and inspiration. For instance, people who share hobbies, fitness, football matches or other interests with you. They can also be people that you spend time with because you're interested in their view of the world and you value their advice. You won't find them naturally in your clan or hoard, so you go out of your way to spend time with them.

It goes without saying that people can drift between the three groups, appear in all three or leave entirely. Many muses can become hoard members who then have the potential, over time, to become clan members. Everyone moves on a spectrum. That's why your forest list must be flexible.

It's important to realize that this forest already exists and you can walk into it immediately (… but ideally finish this chapter first!). So let's move away from the doom and gloom of the first chapters and realize we have everything that we need right in front of us. I don't need to quit my job and go and join some far-flung commune (and neither do you). Instead, we can start living a more awakened life within the life that we've already created for ourselves. Once I stuck my head out of my last rabbit hole adventure, I was almost jubilant with joy. It was a real BOOOOOOM moment! And something we'll explore in much more detail.

When you're doing the exercise at the end of this chapter, you must pay particular attention to the roughly, top five names each category as well as the ones that might be in the process of transitioning between groups. These people represent the trees that stand the closest to you in your forest. In other words, these are the people with whom you have the deepest connection. They're the ones who give you the deepest sense of purpose and joy. Therefore, they need to be always celebrated, but especially during challenging times. From my observations, people with whom you can spend hours chatting via online video calls during the COVID-19 lockdowns are naturally in the 15 mentioned above. A lot of articles have been written about the number of people who've witnessed a significant shift in their social landscape, which is terrific and much needed good news.

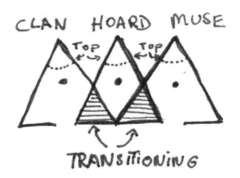

With that in mind, I invite those of you who found themselves scratching their heads because their forest has far too few or too many trees, or who felt claustrophobic or generally uncomfortable with the idea of being dependent on a forest and were much happier with the stand-alone idea of their tree, to continue this journey with me.

Why Boundaries Matter

Men in particular, please keep on reading. And yes, sharpen your pencil yet again!

For this section, you might need to bring a little "sitzfleisch"!

Sitzfleisch is the best German word ever. Directly translated it means "sitting meat". It's something you wish someone when that person has to undergo something that will take a while and isn't very exciting. You're wishing them stamina, endurance and perseverance.

I'm going to take you on a safari through your forest to check your boundaries. Speak to any rancher, farmer, president and even your brain, and you'll hear that boundaries are crucial to a safe and healthy environment, like your forest. Boundaries are like our own skin; they keep out, and allow in what doesn't and does belong! But our skin can't protect us if we neglect it. It's one of the largest organs in our body, and it needs a lot of TLC that requires time and energy. Much the same, protecting and maintaining boundaries cost ranchers, farmers and governments a lot of time, energy and resources.

Physical boundaries have four functions and are set up to select:

1. What stays out
2. What stays in
3. What's allowed in
4. What's allowed out

While it might not be rocket science, it occurred to me that many of my personal boundaries (especially as a man) have been set for me by society and I've accepted them without question. Also, when I was going through my resentment exercise, I realized that some of my boundaries were set by people early on in life, probably when my brain was still absorbing everything without question. In hindsight and on reflection, some were likely not set with intention but came about as a consequence.

Now get your "sitting meat" ready as we walk through the different type of boundaries that you need to be aware of. Don't feel bad that you might not know this stuff; I didn't either until I spent time sitting on my meat in front of the shaman.

It was a real "look at what I've done!" moment!

Boundaries

Boundaries are essential to mental health and wellbeing. We must be able to create boundaries in our interactions with society at large and with the people directly around us. We also connect with the earth and every living thing around us.

These boundaries function in two ways — to make contact and to withdraw or protect.

To live a well-balanced life, we must learn when and how to connect or remove ourselves from the world around us. Both contact and withdrawal are essential to function healthily. However, there can be times when our contact gets distorted, and we're either unaware or don't know how to change.

The mind is potent! It can create multiple coping mechanisms to restrict contact using various distractions, interruptions, resistance and disturbances. These coping mechanisms often develop in times of distress or suffering. As much as this can be positive in helping us survive in difficult times, it can also become a problem if it becomes the norm in our mental processing. When that happens, the distortions created to cope start to prohibit our mental awareness and progress. This is called the *"Contact Boundary Phenomena"*.

During my travels, I've come into contact with many different types of people who've deployed various coping mechanisms to protect themselves (including myself, of course!). Often, they've been through challenging situations, so they either build an emotional wall around themselves or shut their minds down to things they don't want to see or encounter, or do the exact opposite. So, I've found that there are five major contact boundary obstructions or disturbances. Understanding them and being able to figure which are affecting our lives is our first baby step towards building a healthy forest around us.

5 Kinds Of Contact Boundary Disturbances

To ensure our survival, we must make contact with the environment. But how we make contact is guided and ultimately decided by our boundaries. The function of boundaries is to be firm enough to differentiate the Self from others while simultaneously still being open enough to make contact with them. In this process, the individual adapts nourishment from the environment and rejects that which isn't nourishing. Therefore, differentiated contact naturally leads to healthy development. We set these boundaries very early in our lives, so it's essential (similar to our North Star values) that they're set at a level of intensity that protects but also nourishes.

1. **Introjection**

   This is the tendency to accept the beliefs and the standards of others without question or assimilation and to make them congruent with who we are. Taking information in, without critical examination, is a sign of a mental inability to connect with and know oneself. When we do this, we become overly compliant and adaptable to an ever-changing societal structure.

   These people remind me of a chameleon. What is the actual skin color of a chameleon? Do you know? Does anyone know? I know I don't. On the surface, the chameleon's ability to blend with any environment is pretty cool. However, in people, it gets to a point where they can only be defined by their external environment.

They lose touch and contact with themselves because they've spent so much time being defined by what other people say or think about them.

They've swallowed every message whole, without grasping it thoroughly, and they then use it as their own. This can be as a result of authority forcing ideas on us. When this happens, we develop hostility towards the person or institution that pressurized us. This unresolved conflict affects self-control. Over time, this disturbance can lead to a character split inner dialog between the kingpin and loser. The kingpin is blameless, controlling, high-minded, harsh, oppressive and unscrupulous. The loser, on the other hand, plays the role of victim by being cautious, apologetic, helpless and fragile and by assuming powerlessness. This is the passive side of the mind that is without responsibility and prefers to find excuses. Sadly, some of these values are often absorbed in childhood. So for example, if a kid was raised in an environment where things other than the raising of the kid was deemed more important, a lack of self-value will manifest within the Self and will form part of the person's self-belief. In the years to come, these can form retroflections (more on that later).

One way we can discover what isn't part of the true Self is to recall the original (repressed) sense of repulsion and the need to reject or spit out what we swallowed. To unburden ourselves of introjects in our personality, we must deepen awareness of the moral rules, opinions, prejudices and attitudes we accept as normal. If they leave a bad taste, we must spit them out!

Does this sound like you? Often these can quickly be spotted in the resentment therapy homework you did at the beginning of the book.

There's nothing positive about interjection since everything we're presented with should pass through a filter, identifying it as being either good or bad for us, or a combination of the two. Just absorbing is very dangerous for self-care because everything should be challenged or at least scrutinized. We also often see this behavior manifest in what we eat or how we nourish our body. But be careful, the pendulum can swing too far. Only allowing people in who are 100% on the same level can lead to very autistic character traits that can feel very jarring.

2. Confluence

Where introjection leaves the chameleon not questioning anything and just blending into the environment it's presented with, in confluence there isn't even a sense of being a chameleon, the Self is absent. The origin of confluence is actually a beautiful state because it features strongly when we are kids. It's from this state and the influx of introjection that we then start creating a sense of the Self. There are moments where people become part of the greater universe or environment — be it through love, intimacy or other transpersonal connections. But these states should never come with the loss of the Self.

If we create confluence by dissolving the contact boundaries without knowing we are doing so, we create a situation where we confuse another with ourselves. We may not be able to distinguish our own thoughts, attitudes or feelings from something or someone else's.

Having no boundaries not only means that we're always off course and not on our own journey of life but we're on everybody else's journey, (effectively we're lost). It can also lead to dangerous situations, especially when we cross the paths with people who are manipulators.

3. **Projection**

Projection is the reverse of the introjection. In projection, we disown certain aspects of ourselves by assigning them to our external environment. Putting our feelings onto others can lead to paranoia. It's a personal trait, attitude or feeling that isn't experienced for what it is but instead ascribed to someone. It's experienced as being directed at the person projecting rather than something they're doing. Projection, at the right levels, can show up as being highly intuitive and being able to sense something about someone else. But once it's out of balance, we can believe that we can see something that's just a mirror of past trauma.

The person projecting is unaware of what they're doing to others and, instead, believes that it's being done to them. It develops as a defense against conflict and pressure that we don't want to confront. Although we are aware of the issue, we can't envisage stating it openly, so we assume it must be coming from others and lose the sense that we're feeling the impulse.

A perfect example of paranoid projection is the jealous spouse or partner. If you're inclined to jealousy, spend some time in introspection to check if you aren't stifling the desire to be unfaithful or have a deep-seated introjection towards fear of loss, separation or rejection. The jealous partner's repressed feeling causes them to conjure up the notion that their partner is attracted to someone else, and imagines them together or being left behind.

Therefore, without feeling any responsibility in the situation, the jealous party sees themselves as the victim of betrayal. It's a self-denial process where we blame everything that's not going our way on society or our environment. As we know there is no animal that tries to change the environment to look like itself; only the human mind can do that!

We must realize that we are a creative contributor in our environment and are responsible for our reality. Blame achieves nothing, but taking responsibility means that we either introduce change or allow things to stay as they are.

4. **Retroflection**

Retroflection is a process where we turn on ourselves. As I said earlier, it usually starts with introjection that matures to bear fruit as a retroflection.

You see, to retroflex means to "turn sharply back against". Psychologically, retroflection causes withheld emotions, self-punitive anger and severe frustration. Also often referred to the inner-voice, it often manifests with "you should" or "you shouldn't"! It's best friends with anxiety, shame and guilt. Going back to the example of the neglected kid, as an adult, this person's personality and decision making will be steered by value generation. Which in itself isn't a bad thing but will never end up actually nourishing the individual, because the person has an innate value already. The adult version of the kid finds itself in a constant catch 22 of self-sabotage.

In extreme cases, this can also manifest in self-numbing and self-harming behaviors.

It frequently stems from childhood when we lose out against an unsympathetic or tougher environment. The behaviors take hold and stay into our adult years. We don't realize that we're now bigger, stronger and have rights that kids are often deprived. Our circumstances have improved, making it worth having another try at getting what we need from the environment!

Since retroflection is an aggression towards the Self, it's relatively easy to reach through our awareness. That makes it easy to gain control of and automatically recover the blocked impulses, which can then be expressed and removed. Unfamiliar feelings and aggressions may resurface, but we can slowly learn to tolerate and use them constructively. Only when we can become aware of our aggressive impulses can we learn to put them to constructive use. Until then, they will continue to be misused.

With all of these, discovery can begin by recognizing and accepting that we "take it out on ourselves". That creates awareness of the emotions within the retroflecting area of our personality, and the basic outward impulse will emerge. We can then redirect it into healthy expression, as it's singled out and allowed to catch up with the adult areas of our personality. These restorative approaches can increase self-care, self-awareness and introspection.

Retroflections also include what we wanted from others but failed to obtain. We then turn to giving it to ourselves. Unmet needs we wanted to be filled can include attention, love, pity, punishment or other relational needs that cannot realistically be met by yourself.

5. Deflection

Deflection is the process of distraction or veering off so that it's challenging to maintain a sustained sense of contact. As a result, we're actively distancing ourselves from our feelings and those of others. This is often a sign that our defense mechanisms are turned on to very high alert because we had to learn to turn them on as a form of self-protection. It's here where one needs to tread very carefully. Rather than disregarding the armor, we have to view it with gratitude for the protection it's provided to us to date. It's there for a reason. It is only with time and trust that we can put down that shield of armor and show vulnerability in daily life. Often people with high deflection behavior can put their armor to good use in situations. Individuals that like to deflect are highly skilled in easing tension, taking a break and creating a sense of safety.

If you recognize any of these boundary disturbances in yourself, you must note them down. These things will get woven into your goal setting at the end of the book as you start tending to your forest. Some of you might have discovered no fences but fortified barricades that you probably are already very familiar with, but you might now see them in a new light. This also rings true for those of you who've been driving for hours with no fence in sight and found yourself 50 forests removed from your own, trying to find your way back.

Boundaries are a sign of self-care and that others form part of your self-care. It's essential to maintain a healthy balance in your forest of 150 trees because they're all an extension of you.

Boundaries Influence All Our Interactions

Your boundaries become visible as soon as you connect with others. If they're too rigid and inflexible, or too porous and open, people will read them as a sign of how to interact with you. This becomes especially important when it comes to subconscious cues like body language, spoken language, eye contact and even how you present yourself. You see, everything is **vibrational energy**. This **principle** embodies the truth that nothing rests, everything is in motion, and everything **vibrates**. Matter, energy and even spirit are merely varying degrees of **vibration** and these boundaries broadcast how you vibrate.

Fine-tuning and aligning the boundaries in your forest will be one of the biggest jobs in the first year of your journey of self-discovery. If they're set wrongly, it could mean that what's in your forest isn't quite right or in alignment at the moment!

You might think that it seems like a lot of hard work and yes, you're right. The good things in life are often free, but regrettably don't just fall from trees (unless they're rotten to the core). Don't worry, though, it's much like with anything that you get good at — suddenly it gathers its own momentum, and you enjoy being an expert. Besides being good at it, the actual act of connecting with what is most important to you will come with its own joys. Without deep diving into which chemicals get released when you're in positive social settings, you'll very quickly realize that those people you see the most frequently should be those who have a positive effect on you.

Above and beyond how they can nourish and nurture you in various ways, you, in turn, will give them what they need, so the mutually beneficial cycle will continue. I want you to imagine your forest community with 150 positive engaging conversational and connecting loops. A place of safety and resources where you can live out your innate strengths and find support in your weaker moments. Besides healthy boundaries, finding your purpose in your forest is something we'll tackle in the following chapter.

Only by really tending to our forest of people do we have a chance to loosen the grip that the old system has on us because we're not that vulnerable anymore. We might lean less into the services that we depend on from the system as we find them within our forest. The first, and most apparent, is time, or rather the lack of time we suffer from. By pulling together with your clan and hoard, you can trade time with each other by sharing tasks and freeing time for one another and for your muse.

This trade can be as simple to asking your neighbor or friend to cook a larger dinner to share with your family because you have pressing commitments. In turn, you can do the same for them at a later date or help them out in some other way. "I'll do

Halloween if you do Easter" types of exchange. Exchanges also extend to hand-me-downs, sharing tools and being emotionally available when you can see the need.

This banality might not seem visionary, and it shouldn't because it's that obvious and we crave it. Of course, there's a momentary dopamine rush when you source that perfect t-shirt from a big-brand online retailer and click "buy". Then there's the wave of excitement when it then finally arrives. However, there's nothing more nourishing for the soul than seeing another kid running around with a t-shirt that your kid has worn. Not only because it reminds you of the memories of your kid growing-up, but also because in your heart of hearts, you knew that the t-shirt wasn't done yet when your kid outgrew it. Seeing another little person wearing it while tearing around and discovering life connects you with the bigger community that you're part of. You've spared the environment from producing yet another t-shirt as well. Our forests are a bedrock for emotional, financial and environmental sustainability.

Besides the micro economy of trade, we'll also go into the exchange of your natural gifts and the sense of purpose it brings. What's really important about reconnecting to your people in positive, nurturing ways is that it's within these communities that we can heal and build strategies for the traumas and crises that we're all facing and will continue to face. As a tight knight community, we're in a much better position to tackle the emotional complexity around wounds of oppression, segregation and supporting people who've been displaced. It's within these forests that we'll heal the old and find strategies for the future world. As it stands, the big macro systems are driving the strategies of the future, and it's within our power to show them that community living is at the core of that strategy.

Exercise

Put aside a bit of time and get yourself a pen and paper. Have your resentment therapy exercise at hand too because you'll be surprised to see many of the same names there that will also feature in your forest. Don't be surprised or question yourself. It's often the people who we care the most about that can leave the deepest scars.

Write down these three headings: **Clan**, **Hoard** and **Muse** and start writing names down. If some people straddle more than one category, list them in each but only count them as one. Remember, there's no absolute hard science around the 150 but give it your best go. You'll see that the further you push, the deeper you walk into your forest. Just because you haven't been in touch with somebody for a while doesn't mean they're not an essential part of your 150, it's just that they don't jump out at you right away. I like to encourage people to use their social media connections in this exercise too. Although some will make it onto your list, at the same time you might start questioning why others are actually there.

Dunbar recommends we use that *"impromptu meeting at the bar"* as an indicator of who belongs on our 150-list. Unfortunately, if you're anything like me, that advice gets tricky because I'll speak to every and anybody at a bar, so try this: a person who you'd feel comfortable, and even excited with, if they surprisingly sat next to you on a plane for a quick 30-minute flight... for those of you who are afraid of flying go with: find yourself caught with under a tree whilst escaping the rain.

Anyway, push through as far as you can with that list. Keep in mind that you can always add and remove at a later stage. Once you're done, give stars to those who rank in the top five, six or seven on each list. If you find that difficult, try imagining who you could be stuck in a lift with for over an hour — maybe that will help shorten the list.

Because we're all different, we might not have an equal mathematical spread across all three categories, or the five listed muses might seem unfair in comparison to the five listed as clan. You'll eventually find a means of fairness, but for now, just ensure that you have some representation under each heading.

These people are at the core of your wellbeing and represent the trees that grow the closest to you in your forest. Their wellbeing must be as vital to yours and should feature highly in planning and goal setting when you get to do your Elementalist exercise.

CHAPTER

6

PURPOSE AND FLOW

Ladies and gentlemen, this is it — where it all comes together!

You need to spend a bit of time on this chapter, so if you're reading this between running errands or waiting for something, or even reading on the loo — maybe it's not the best moment to continue. You need a good 30 minutes as most of this chapter is an exercise.

I hope you have all your prior homework at hand. If not, go and get it because you can't continue without it.

While I was researching what kind of coming-of-age message I want to give my kids, it became more evident and more apparent with every rabbit hole that I managed to work my way through. Of course, you want your kids to be happy in their future life. But because today's maximum consumer-consumption version of happiness is on such a slippery slope and so fraught with danger, the word "responsibility" popped up immediately. It was like happiness and the notion of responsibility were identical twins conjoined at the hip. Instantly I realized that any advice I had to give felt very old school: "you should do this and that, BUT..." and up came the old instructive finger of what not to do. Surely there were less draconian approaches?

It was only when I was in Lapland that it dawned on me that **purpose** was what I was trying to teach them. Purpose is the one thing that has a direct and immediate feedback loop to the people who surround you. It nurtures you and others! And it was within that nurturing where I discovered the safety net I was looking for. The more I explored and became aware of nurturing, the more I suddenly found it popping up everywhere. Nurturing money is only going to give you more of that (and darn, don't get me wrong, we all need money in our pockets) but maybe we should also add things that come directly from the source rather than always attaching a financial transaction to it. Once I discovered that and knew it rang true, it became my North Star for my research (...and possibly for my midlife crise!).

What's my purpose, or that of my people… or us as a species?

Yup exactly — it was one of those moments!

Right at the beginning of the book, I asked you to jump: well if you did, this is the chapter where you have the potential to land!

So I hope that by now you have gathered your notes and thoughts and have in hand:

- Your true North Star value and possibly a few sub-values.

- The list of names of the top 20 connections in your forest. (Make sure you have at least one name per group. If you don't have a clan, hoard or muse in your top 20 list, then list someone who might not be part of your top 20 but is at the top of that group.)

- The element(s) that you feel represents you the most (ideally — especially the wind and earth people — have the words within the elements that spoke to you the most rather than the name of the element. You already know why!)

Finding Your Purpose

Here's how easy it is. Draw three triangles next to each other and label them separately as **clan**, **hoard** and **muse**.

Now do the following (and please stick to the structure as it has a certain magic to it):

On the **bottom right**, write down only the element(s) and/ or the words that you associate closely with yourself. Do that for all three triangles. Those of you that have more than one specific element might already find that the elements will start to divide depending on the forest. If you only have one, that's absolutely okay too. Each element has different aspects to it, so see if anything specific pops up in each group. For example, a person that has wind and water might find that when with the clan they are more water and when with the hoard more wind etc.

Once you have distributed your elements than we can move on!

So here we go:

(Complete one triangle at a time — not all three at the same time.)

Triangle 1:

Ask yourself the following questions again (they might seem familiar by now, but there are slight changes!).

Start writing your answers down staring from the top of the triangle and then moving anti-clockwise:

Top:

1. **Who am I?** Answer with your North Star/values and write them down, pick your favorite one today for this group and list it as an (A) bullet point.

2. **What do I love to do?** Write down the thing you most like to do for mind, body and heart. You might find that when seen across the three triangles, you want to add/change what you love to do considering the three groupings. Continue to list them in bullet points **(B) mind, (C) body** and **(D) heart**.

Bottom Left:

3. **Who do I do it for?** List the names of the people you do things for. Remember, we are exploring the top 20 names, but if you want to write more, or less, or add somebody new — go ahead.

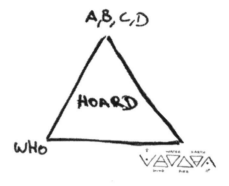

Bottom Right: (Where you've already listed the elements)

4. **What do they want or need, and how can my natural traits (6-elements) help them attain this?** See if you need to answer this question individually by name or if there's a larger pattern that you can identify in this group.

5. **How do they change as a result?** There's no wrong or right here; it's about being aware of your answer. You're not responsible for their change. It's more about how you contribute to their inevitable change through your presence and natural traits. So rather, it's you being a catalyst for their transformation. Again, you can do it by name or as a general pattern.

Next, I want you to condense all your thoughts that are currently running through your mind and refine and combine them into a single word. Again the word that you come up with needs to only make sense to you. If one word is too difficult, try finding a concept or idea.

Write it into the middle of the triangle as bullet (E).

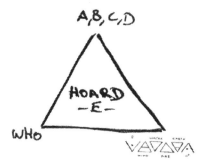

Move on to the next triangle and do the same, and then continue to the third one. Don't dwell on your answers for too long; just keep moving on. If you find that these three triangles are too confining, draw more but write beneath them why you're adding another one because it will help you later when you revisit your work.

All done!

I now want you to draw another triangle and write the points listed under (E) at each of the three points of the triangle. Don't worry if they're all the same. As you write them down you might want to tweak them here and there since seeing them all together might trigger something. Think, be aware and have fun with it!

Welcome to the holy trinity of your life purpose!

If you instinctively sense that you want to combine it all into one major purpose at the center of the triangle, feel free to do so.

Then — yes, you've guessed it, get your phone and record yourself answering the exact questions you've just written down.

Carefully listen to your replies and also check in with what your pilot is saying whilst doing so. Once you've recorded and listened to your responses to each triangle, go back and listen very closely to your original recording.

Expect there to be a difference in the details and accuracy between the two exercises. Also, hear how this version is far more aligned to your true self and less of an imprint of society's "married father of two" version.

That's how much awakening you've been able to achieve in just a couple of pages.

This is what gets me so excited — how much clearer we can see with a little bit of groundwork.

You've come so far in such a short time. Imagine where this could take you if you weave this into your daily life and ritualize an annual check-in to see how you've progressed and developed. Plus, you have the recordings and paperwork to record the change happening in front of your eyes, just like the changing seasons.

It's not uncommon for some of your pilots to be kicking and screaming in the background while all this is going on; ignore it and just let it happen behind the scenes. Some of you might feel deflated as the results might not be what you expected or aspire to.

The reality is that 'purpose' has been so overestimated that we often believe our purpose to be much bigger, more glamorous and harder to reach than it really is. For a few, there is a grand purpose, and they go on to win a Nobel Prize. But honestly, who in the top 20 of your 150 connections relies on your presence with a Nobel Prize in hand?

Purpose is hidden just beneath the surface, and regrettably, it's rarely as glamorous as "save the world". It sits quietly and powerfully just under our nose within reach of our awareness. Thanks to today's information highway and generally supersized mindset, we're just unable to see it since we're trying to find it with our modern filters of grandeur. Our commodity-driven attitude where we can buy anything we want without accessing value from within further hampers our efforts to find our life purpose. Finally, the fact that we've also disconnected from our community elders as a base for intergenerational wisdom with a deep-rooted understanding of purpose is the final barrier to ever finding our purpose and true value and meaning to our lives. There are many articles online about the regrets people experience when they're on their deathbed, and the themes are often very similar. It's usually a regret that they could have connected and incorporated so much earlier on in their lives if they hadn't been so separated from society. ● <u>Palliative Care Nurse, Bonnie Ware</u>

Living with true purpose within one's tight knit forest is something that could arguably be today's rarest commodity in the WEIRD tribe. Miraculously it's free of charge and innately ours! If embraced and played out on a grand scale, it has the capacity to allow us to loosen the grip of the existing system.

Too cryptic? Let's walk through an example to make it a bit clearer.

The Connection Between Purpose And Flow

Some people strike gold early in life and have learnt to own their purpose and make the wise decision to really lean into it. Generally, we can easily pick people out from the crowd who've found their purpose. They feel very comfortable in their skin, own their own space and you literally can't imagine them doing anything else if you were to ask for a different outcome for them.

Take my wife, for example — one of her purposes in her forest is to attentively and compassionately listen. And when she's fully leaning into that purpose, she has no other option than to start self-actualizing. As a result, the more she actualizes, the more she reaches flow — and as with any flow states, she reaches her most engrossed, ecstatic yet sustainable levels of energy. Here's the beauty of it — not only does it give her flow, but it also helps her form deep-rooted and nourishing connections in her community that sustain and protect her, and simultaneously helps the community stick together intimately. The more the community can rely on her purpose, the more other people can hone in on their own purpose. Besides, people who are in flow beam out an infectious energy and inspire others to find their flow (also referred to as mirroring) — thus moving the forest into a fuller state of flow.

Forest members that are in flow are esteemed as highly valued fellows of the community, making them focus even more on their purpose and become community experts within the purpose that presents itself. Becoming experts within your forest makes you an intrinsic part of the fabric of the group, freeing up and energizing other members to do the same. As I've said it before, we as humans, mirror and merge with each other right down to the vibrational level of the people close to us. A bit like instruments that you start tuning in to the same frequency.

The more forest members self-actualize through purpose and reach flow, the more the community will start trading their purposes amongst themselves. It's the beginning, once again, of a purpose-driven commodity trade or barter system that's kept tribal cultures alive for millennia. It's one of the underlying origins of our first economic systems and a reason why humanity has been able to make it this far. I think the time is right to re-embrace something that's so innately part of us and empower change at grass root level today. The more we utilize the skills and resources available within our forest the more we can loosen the grip the macro systems have on us.

Now having just completed the last exercise it might come as no surprise that with your new awareness you might not be that happy with how your purpose aligns with your forest and its boundaries. Whether your purpose comes as a surprise or you're already aligned to it, awakening is moving from one state to another. Finding our purpose isn't a one-off thing though, because we evolve and mature, and as we do so, our purpose adapts. Life is in a state of constant flux, ebb and flow and evolution. Therefore, we must remain continually and curiously aware and set intent aligned with our state.

If you feel like you've currently missed the mark in life, don't worry! This process isn't about tearing down the system — life has to happen, and there's a lot in life that isn't that much fun or aligned with who we are. Back in Africa, a vital but tedious daily chore was to go and fetch the water. Often it took a very long time to get to the water, secure your spot in the long queue and then carry the heavy container back home. In many tribes, people walked together singing songs, exchanging gossip and playing makeshift games with rocks in the sand as they waited their turn.

A Rabbit Hole Perspective Of Flow

I mentioned flow earlier, and I'd love to quickly take you down a rabbit hole into states of flow because it's the epitome of joy.

The concept of flow has existed for thousands of years. However, in the 1970s a ● Hungarian psychologist, Mihaly Csikszentmihalyi, became fascinated by artists who became so lost in their creative work that they'd lose track of time and even ignore food, water and sleep. Through his research, he noticed similar experiences with scientists, athletes, and authors. It was a state of hyper-focus and complete engagement that he described as "optimal experience." He, together with other researchers including Jeanne Nakumara, with came up with the Flow Theory. At its core, they identified five factors that are vital for achieving a state of flow.

1. It needs to be a task that you find intrinsically rewarding.

2. You need clear goals and a sense of progress.

3. The task needs clear and immediate feedback.

4. The challenge must match the perceived skills. (This requires a sense of personal control or agency over the task.)

5. It must require an intense focus on the present moment.

Further research found that these optimal states of consciousness can be found in everyday activities with everyday people too; tasks as simple as washing dishes or sweeping the garden. In fact, over 65% of Americans recognize that they feel that state "sometimes". That's what was happening in Africa with the people undertaking the tedious task of fetching water every day. By making it a community activity and engaging in small things that they enjoyed along the way, they could turn it into a pleasant experience and speed up time while doing so (time distortion is a significant element of flow).

Connecting with your environment and its people with intent, deploying your skills to the task or asking somebody to step in for you in exchange for you doing something for them with your skill set is at the crux of this. Science has found that people find flow at work much more frequently than in their relaxing downtime, even if the work isn't in alignment with their interests. And people who work with other people on specific tasks with measurable and clear milestones tend to move through the more tedious parts of the job with a higher sense of purpose that doesn't necessarily align with the actual task at hand. Why? Because the information feedback loops aren't framed in a negative mindset of "I really hate my job", but are more in line with "if we get through this bit in XYZ time, with my input of (E) here, and that person's skill of doing that (F), then we can (B,C,D) later". So although you're engaged with the process of earning a wage, you've changed the playing field from clock watching — "when can I get out of here" thinking to —"how do I deploy my skills" and more importantly live my life wherever I am and whatever I am doing.

Self-awareness is critical to program states of flow wherever possible. The more aware you are, the more you can bring joy into the now, and with more self-awareness you start making different decisions for yourself and your forest, who in turn will also do the same, and so the Mexican wave of cascading change begins!

Remember, we can't buy happiness, and happiness from external things can't wash away your misery (well, maybe for a moment, before the despair rears its ugly head again). Happiness and joy are inside jobs. Our identity becomes a façade when we define it around external trappings. Nothing in life will ever have meaning unless you give it meaning from within yourself! The secret is to accept the mundane without question and then adapt your mindset and actions to make it an enjoyable experience. What we think, we become — so approaching situations with dread, apathy, or fear puts you in a negative frame of mind which will make things worse. Approaching the situation positively and finding ways to enjoy it empowers you and brings joy and happiness. What I'm saying is that you don't want to be the effect, but rather the cause; when you give value, you get value in return.

Another thing that brings people down is expectation. Nothing in life is promised or guaranteed, and no one owes you anything. When you start making positive contributions, even at a micro level, you'll see the same coming back your way. Life exists where you put your energy, and if you can't control where your energy goes you can't be present or concentrate. Once you can grasp that you must create value in life, then you're in control of your life. Take responsibility, serve through value, serve through purpose, and you'll find yourself in the driver's seat of your purpose, joy and flow.

When you've found that space of understanding and responsibility, external events and systems won't control you. They might impact your life or affect your body and mind, but they won't shake your foundations. You can choose how to frame external information. View it in the light of your values and purpose, always looking for ways that you can contribute rather than react.

You are then operating from a place of abundance rather than a place of scarcity.

Find the happiness in each moment; and learn to let go peacefully. What you resist will persist. Flow is actually about subtle forcefulness and willingly surrendering to a situation.

For example, if you get caught in a strong water current, your survival depends on letting go and allowing yourself to get carried by the force around you; if you resist and try to swim against the current, you'll get tired and could drown.

Today, we're torn between financial responsibility, institutions, consumption, lack of time and the occasional fun times through the form of product-laden hobbies and nightlife. They're all part of an external monopoly game of life... and that is all it is — just a game!

Are you the person who wants to get exploited, or the person who recognizes that whilst external things can be entertaining, meaningful reward however comes from living in and serving your community in the here and now?

Focus and concentrate on chaos mindfully. Get to understand polarity — having opposing thoughts simultaneously. Don't lean too far into any thought or concept — neutrality is okay. Unfortunately, patriarchy and the resulting hyper-masculinity has created the rigid lines of right and wrong and obliterated anything in between.

Your awareness and purpose within your own environment are strong enough to create change at a macro level. The macro systems are readying themselves for change as well, but before they map out the future in isolation, it's pivotal to have awakened consumers directing what world they want to consume. There can be a world ahead of us where huge macro business and economies can support the need for community and sustainability.

There's this phenomenal ancient Zulu tribal expression that perfectly encapsulates what took me an entire book to say!

Ubuntu - "I am because you are!"

If we live this from our hearts and through our purpose, then the system will start to mirror, but it's up to us to set the tone.

CHAPTER

7

THE POWER OF RITUAL AND
THE ELEMENTALIST

In short, this chapter will tell you how to have BBQs all year round and to make sure you bring your own special sauce along!

In all seriousness, though, in our long distant past, we spent much more of our time connecting mind, body and heart to activities within our communities to create something bigger than ourselves. Thanks to the conditioning of our commodity-driven world, ancient rituals that we still lean into are all about consumption! What do I want for my birthday, Christmas, what did you get at Easter and trick or treating? It's not surprising that traditions like Lent, where you actually make sacrifices, have become less popular since they do little for the bottom line.

But the good news is that these traditions are still here and can be used as anchors. There are plenty of rituals and traditions from eternities ago that still exist. They're hidden in our language, how and what we eat, the way we socialize (I mean why do we go to clubs or have full moon parties?). Strangely enough, we're all still very aware of the full moon, but besides possible sleep disturbances, it doesn't really add much to our lives.

The reason why shadows of our ancient behaviors are still around is that they are so perfectly suited to us as social creatures who have the capacity to connect to larger concepts (especially transcendence of time) and bind them to our environment. That's one of the reasons why traditional religions that became established over the last 2,000 years have started to miss the mark for many, especially the WEIRD tribe. Part of the problem with many of the mass indoctrination type religions is that their core is based around tales, stories and historical facts that have little resonance with the environment and socio-economic backdrop that we have to navigate today. And that's led to a vast increase in alternative spirituality.

I'm a big believer in not reinventing the wheel; use what's already there as a foundation or framework for something that will help serve us better. This doesn't only include religions, technology and business infrastructure that surrounds us, but all festivals and traditions that we already celebrate at home or are exposed to as well. From there we can create new customs that we can share with other people.

Growing up as a kid who learned and embraced a multitude of cultures, and now raising 'third-culture kids' (children who grow up in places that are not their parents' homeland), we've needed to become super flexible. In our household its Christmas right now and we're incorporating the tradition of the Netherlands where the height of Christmas is on the 6thof December (Sinterklaas, or Saint Nicholas), whilst also including the continental European celebration on the evening of the 24th, plus the British 25thcustom into our festivities. And I know we're not the only ones; the third-culture tribe is the fastest growing tribe in the world, not only in the WEIRD tribe but globally. This trend will continue to grow as our economies become globalized, and the workforce becomes more mobile. Skilled people will increasingly network and traverse the globe, and because of the unequal distribution of wealth, there will continue to be an influx of refugees across continents as well. It's unlikely that these patterns will change and it will ultimately result in us coming together as a truly international society where traditions will meld, and separation will become blurred. Just in my kids' school alone, the festive season between Halloween and New Year's Day is insane (Hanukkah, Diwali, Thanksgiving, Guy Fawkes day, Saint Nicholas advents, Saint Lucia and, of course, everything that goes with Christmas).

This all makes me consider myself extremely lucky because it helps my family and me to learn to set up camp very quickly in every country we arrive in. We understand the power of these rituals and the communities that surround them. And being in the presence of people who connect to a higher conviction that they express through food, song, dance, and laughter is a compelling experience. In fact, even without understanding the cultural context or even the language, you feel your spirits rise, and mood lift.

Practicing different rituals is part of our embodiment of community and needs to be brought more to the foreground for the multitude of reasons we've discussed so far. Thanks to the growth of third-culture people, there's more and more research into the effects. One area of development has been specific mindfulness techniques (don't get me wrong it's a growing movement, but moving countries is a really tough thing to do. As I've told you, I've done it eight times — just thinking about it makes me want to call that therapist, again!)

These new mindfulness techniques focus on building routines and rituals within existing schedules as you bed down and grow roots in your new country, especially if you arrive with kids. One of the striking findings in research data is that creating a culture and a sense of belonging through rituals allows people to connect to something greater than themselves. Whether it's a routine, tradition or value, it will enable us to be part of something bigger which gives us this sense of connection. And it needn't be something elaborate; it can be as simple as making Sunday roast a tradition or taking a post-dinner walk in the forest a routine. The fact that these newly created routines and rituals are helping third-culture families settle more easily in their new lives proves that it's never too late to start a new purpose-driven practice helping you arrive in a new place even if you stayed stationary.

And to help you arrive in your new world, I have created a seasonal time chart within which you can embed your journey of self-discovery.

Welcome To The Elementalist

Today, in the WEIRD tribe, disposable time can be as scarce as disposable income. Therefore I've created the Elementalist with the foresight that you won't stick to it; you'll make an enthusiastic start, and then most probably will be side tracked. But the important thing is that when your awareness finally catches up with you and you are riddled with guilt, the Elementalist will offer you an exact and seamless entry point to re-engage with your journey. This process, as the Elementalist, doesn't really have a beginning or an end, and, yes, Rome wasn't built in a day.

We're going to focus on three ritual centers that divide into six thanks to human's magical powers of cognitive time travel:

a) Your North Star (now and tomorrow)

b) Your tree of life (now and tomorrow)

c) Your forest (now and tomorrow)

We'll piggyback existing seasonal festivals that are already deeply rooted in tradition and are most probably already earmarked in your annual calendar, so don't worry too much about having to innovate from scratch (... that shouldn't stop some of you having a field day with this).

Some of you might view the Elementalist as too esoteric and alternative because its deeply rooted in the natural cycles of nature. Feel free just to use your calendar or the dates promoted by big business to encourage consumerism. You might, however, discover on closer inspection that even they follow natural cycles and are also deeply impacted by them. For example, do you know that more and more research is showing that lunar cycles impact the stock markets? ◉

The main reason why the Elementalist leans into the natural cycles is because it solidifies our journey to not only reconnect to our own mind, body, heart and community, but also with the world that we live in. It also gives parents the chance to teach their kids how to connect to the natural rhythms around us, opening them up to the wonderment of the natural world that surrounds us. (Don't opt for apps — doing it through technology keeps us locked in our minds again, and to reconnect we have to ideally embody the calendar differently.)

It's also one of the main reasons you see so many drawings in this book. Not only because they can form part of a visual language, a shorthand, a shared experience to encourage intergenerational self -discovery, they're also used to compile the

Elementalist. Therefore the whole charts form the foundational time map for self-exploration. You can always return to the different chapters to help unlock any specific symbol you might stumble across within the Elementalist.

So the first thing I want you to do is to get yourself a blank sheet of paper. This page will become your index, your hymn sheet, your coat of arms. For the artistic among you, use symbols or, if you prefer, you can write a bio about all the new things you've discovered.

We're looking for you to include:

- Your North Star by clan, hoard and muse.

- As many names as you like from your forest.

- Things that you really enjoy in mind, body and heart and mark your lead system.

- What combination of the 6-elements you find within yourself. Feel free also to do this by clan, hoard and muse and if possible mind, body and heart.)

- Have your resentment therapy list handy.

- Have your boundary list with you (if the list has changed in different parts of your forest, that's fine.)

This is a great moment!

It's like having the full recipe of who you are and how you tick right in front of you.

Embellish it!

But keep it safe (... like Heinz keeps their ketchup recipe safe!).

Do not restrict yourself in any way here — things might suddenly connect in ways you've never seen. The first time I did this I got slight vertigo. Once I saw everything that seemed very big in my mind's eye put on a piece of paper in front of me, it felt, TIDY, for lack of a better word.

Keep your creation, your secrete sauce recipe — its very important for what we are about to start planning!

It's at this point that I want to introduce you to the visual of the Elemental:

This cardinal map shows movement in space and time. It includes the seasons and the symbols for the 6-elements, the moon cycles, the here and now and the time travel aspect of life, all encompassed by your forest of 150 and the boundaries that you have created for yourself.

Why does it exist? Well, this, in conjunction with your own secrete sauce recipe, is always there waiting for you if you need a quick and easy entry point to re-engage with your journey and annual rhythms if you are taken off course.

Those of you with a scientific mind might say that this looks like a cell. It does, and it's been designed like that intentionally. The cell is a perfect symbol that the universe exists within the microcosm that isn't too dissimilar from the macrocosm and vice versa. And that's the thread that runs through this awakening process. It's the awareness that we're not alone; we're all connected and mirror within these connections.

Spirit Walking — The Shaman's Paradigm

Many of us view shamanism as primitive and see no place for it in modern society. Science, on the other hand, is starting to have a change of heart as researchers discover principles supporting the ways ancient cultures accepted and responded to the world around them. To shamans, it isn't only the biotas that are alive; everything is filled with spirit and energy. This concept is called animism. The word is derived from the Latin "anima" meaning air, breath or spirit.

Animists believe that every feature within our environment has an essential essence of spirit as well as awareness. This includes everything from single-celled organisms to insects, fauna, flora, rocks, rivers, mountains and even wind and rain. Shamans know that spirit is the structure within which all physical manifestation gets sustained. Everything exists through and is anchored in spirit. Spirit is also what connects every aspect of the material and tangible realm.

Quantum Physics

Quantum physics views the world as originating in the vibrations created by microscopic superstrings. Each of these indiscernible features can produce a particle of matter. Considered within the patterns of New Physics, this unseen and intangible "unknown" is the connection of all physical reality. All living things, as well as nonliving, are intertwined on the quantum level.

Think of it this way; our physical bodies are composed of elements including calcium, iron, oxygen, sodium and many more. These are the very same raw materials that make up the oceans, soils, mountains and atmosphere of our planet. Ancient societies recognized this long before the advent of modern science.

Every single cell in our body carries the fundamental building blocks of life — DNA. It's made up of an extraordinary double helix-shaped chain of chemical data that determines our physical form. Within the twisting steps of this miniscule molecule lives the story of our human evolution. And here's another fact to show that the ancients were a step ahead of us — every life form, from the most primitive single-celled organisms to giant trees and animals share the same four amino acids in their physical makeup.

Extensive research has discovered that within the 60,000 to 80,000 genes that create our human genome lies the material to create all other forms of life on our planet. Within the complex strands of our DNA is housed not only the blueprint for a human being but an astonishing archive of codes for all other life that shares our world. We have the entire interlinked environment in every single cell.

Apart from being an amazing repository of information, our DNA structure is also a source of measurable energy. Lab studies proved that DNA emits photons in visible light ranges. These photons are totally undetectable to our senses, but they're continually radiating from DNA in every cell. Since photons have no measurable mass, they can travel over vast distances. As a result, energy emitted by our bodies as photons from our DNA combines with that of all other beings with who we come into contact. Remember, all DNA radiates these energy particles; therefore, it occurs in all places as subtle energy connecting all of creation.

So in effect, your invisible DNA-emitted energy is inevitably continually interacting with the unseen energy of all other beings. These ongoing interactions create an unavoidable, but sensational situation; as energy waves contact others, it creates a progressive feedback loop. Through each element in the loop, we invariably affect and are affected by others. The implication is that through interactions with diverse beings, the unseen, glowing part of ourselves has the ability to change and evolve. It doesn't end there, though. Considering that photons continue to move infinitely onward, they can keep developing, interacting and changing, even after the body that produced them perishes.

So modern science is coming back full circle to align with the understanding of the ancient world. When we transfer the scientific information into the perspective of early shamanic belief systems, this subtle energy or vibration translates to spirit. Here's the foundation of shamanism — spirit exists beyond space and time and is endless. It's an undetectable force that forms and permeates the body and also things. It was interesting to hear the shaman speak about our economy and democracy being sick and in need of nurturing. Still, before nurturing them, we have to start with ourselves first.

And quantum physics has proven that the change just within you has the power to change your forest and beyond. So you truly can become the change you want to see!

Back To Our Journey

Sorry for the short detour — now that you have a more in-depth understanding let's commence with our annual journey that lies ahead. In short, the Elementalist is your loose guide to keep you on track, especially when you deviate from your course due to external stressors, and you want to check-in and get back on track. That's when you reach for your self-created secret sauce recipe and place it next to the Elementalist to see where you stand and how to get back onto your envisaged journey.

Nothing more and nothing less!

At the end of the chapter I have also added a text for a self-recording that you can use at any given time to throw you right back into the journey and goal setting (look for Rabbit Hole of Awakening).

This is a flexible process. Pick and choose what you want to implement in your annual Elementalist calendar.

a) **Your North Star (now and tomorrow)**

> **Now:** create a daily ritual for your North Star. Write or draw the words or symbols and hang them somewhere where you conduct daily rituals like making coffee or brushing your teeth. You can also put them a key ring you use daily. My routine is when I'm watering the plants in my flat, I'm also watering my core values in my mind's eye. While I'm doing that, I ask how far removed I am from them, what things might have impacted individual values and is there anything I can do in the here and now to get one step closer to them? (I reward myself as well if I'm still on point). It's at this juncture I'd like to bully you a little. Add the question "what am I grateful for today" to your daily routine. It might not correlate with your North Star values, but

viewing life through the lens of what's good as opposed to negatively instilled values that you might be carrying around with you is a bloody fantastic proactive way to kick off your day. And I really mean it!

Tomorrow: just as with the seasons, sometimes we find ourselves in a season that doesn't want to align with our values. It can be for various reasons. When you notice in your daily practice that you're far off the mark for more extended periods, even when putting in the effort, it's time to move into more long-term planning. Go back to the exercises set in earlier chapters and establish what you don't have enough of or too much of in your life. Backtracking from the macro into micro through the triangles can be really helpful here. If it's an abstract thing like, let's say, security, then find an embodied version of it, lets say money, and start adding it to your lunar goal setting. (This will make more sense later, so don't stress.)

b) **Your tree of life (now and tomorrow)**

Now: clearly, your tree of life (the mind, body and heart) can live in the here and now, but often they get high jacked by the mind and therefore we can dwell in the past or future. Building a practice for your North Star like mentioned above helps to look after the issues of the heart in the here and now. So for your tree of life, I really want you to focus on your body on a daily

basis through breathing. There are hundreds of ways of building awareness around your breathing. You can choose to keep your awareness constant or just when you're practicing meditation, or even going for a walk. You must decide how you can give it your best attention.
● Lucas Rockwood | TEDxBarcelona

Tomorrow: besides the daily routine, allow time during the week to consider what your tree of life needs (what don't you have enough of or too much of?). I used to have a calendar reminder that popped up on a Sunday afternoon asking me "did you have enough fun and laughter this past week?" This question prompted me to think about it, but since it was Sunday, it also gave me a few minutes to plan the week ahead to bring more fun and laughter into my life. Awareness is the most important thing you need to schedule; it will reveal things that you can then act on. Like with the North Star if, for whatever reason, life isn't working out even though you're giving it your full attention, then kick it over to your lunar goal setting.

c) **Focusing on your forest (now and tomorrow)**

Now: once you know what your emotional forest looks like it becomes an easy daily (or for some a Sunday) reflection. Where am I in my forest at the moment and how well surrounded am I in my forest? Also, do a quick boundary check daily to see if any of your boundaries are being crossed or not utilized enough. Having a daily check-in helps you to make small, quick changes to correct anything that's moving out of line. Blurred or distorted boundaries usually make us feel out of touch and often happen in times when life becomes hectic and stressed.

I wanted to quickly remind you of the Zulu concept of Ubuntu — *"I am because you are"*. Always strive to be humble and full of gratitude. Extend it not only to everyone and everything in your environment but to everything you think and feel as well. Shunning or escaping uncomfortable things in life is the wrong thing to do, rather embrace their presence and playfully question their origins. Embrace micro to macro and back again — Ubuntu!

Do this especially within the hoard part of the forest because you never know who might walk into your life today and become a long-term stayer. Sometimes a single encounter can be enough too; not everyone will or needs to stay in your forest to make an impact. As I mentioned previously, it's the part of the forest that can fluctuate continuously — even on a daily basis.

I have an anecdote here (one of my many), but I genuinely love this one. It stands out because I think it might have been too much for some people in my company! My wife, some friends and I were in a taxi from a restaurant to a bar. I sat in front with the taxi driver and rather than ignoring him as many people would do, I asked him how his journey in life got him here and where he was heading. It quickly became in an intense conversation, actually, to such an extent that he accepted my invitation to join us in the bar – despite his religion and job prohibiting him for doing so. The music in the bar was deafening, making conversation difficult, so he finished his orange juice and went on his merry way. That night we didn't only take a taxi — we also met a person. If you adopt this attitude and do it with great intent in life then you don't work or run errands, you're always meeting people and connecting deeply within with your environment. And the beauty about this is that the person who you're meeting, rather than working, is also meeting you. You've changed that moment for both of you through connection. That's the power of living with awareness and intent. It's our choice — you can view it as going to work or as making connections.

Tomorrow: this is where I really come into my own — BBQs, and lots of them! No joking, there are four seasons, and they're littered with social events, festivals, birthdays and, as I said BBQs. This is the activity where you need to invite your forest to come and play. It's how you water your forest and show them how important they are. You might think this is too obvious, and it might be. The difference is going in with intent and knowing how pivotal they are to you. It will change the face of how you prepare and share your festive moments. Also, with more foresight and planning, your forest is alerted in advance that you want to spend time and share a feast with them. This will bring them great joy since the mere act of discussing your plan already creates the cognitive reality that it will happen. They can visualize themselves with you well in advance of the actual event, and that's super important because that's where watering your forest already starts. I use the big four: Christmas, Easter, Halloween and — you guessed it — big summer solstice BBQs. To me, the seasonal change is excellent for spending time outdoors. I use it as time to get my kids to see what elements they think they're made of and if there are any changes as well. It's also a time to reflect on the season that's just gone by and how you managed to clear your goals, as well as set new ones for the next season. I also urge you to tell your forest how you fared and what new goals you have lined up for the following season. Giving your goals verbal presence in these rhythmic gatherings brings your goals into their own — they seem to really manifest! PRESSURE!

It's a bit like the Bo-selfies; they're good moments to take stock from a macro point of view while enjoying the micro. This is an excellent opportunity to remove some of the 200 names from the resentment list, writing them on a sheet of paper and burning it. When I do this I'm letting go of them because I feel ready to release the resentment, forgive and move on!

In my mind, I see this as a space where men can really come into their own too. Knowing how vital your forest is, why not use the powerful energy of the sun to protect your forest and all the rituals that keep it healthy and progressive. So don't just stand by the BBQ, but maybe kick that up a level and pull together with everyone to really master these larger get-togethers and cultural moments.

If, for whatever reason, you find your forest, or parts of it a little empty even though you've put in the effort, it's time to move it along to lunar goal setting.

Okay, so I've spoken a lot of the lunar goal setting. What is it!

Lunar Goal Setting

The lunar cycles are amazing tools that have been used throughout time to keep track of things that don't have a daily cycle, like the sun, or extended cycles, like the seasons. Lunar phases are trackable and visible to the naked eye by the obvious waxing and waning of the moon over 29.5-day cycles. Today's monthly calendar system is based on the lunar cycles structured on days and dates which are out of sync with nature. No surprise there — we're so out of touch overall!

The moon is the perfect natural tool for anything that needs medium-term attention, so I'd like to urge you to set your goals at the new moon with the intention to achieve them at the full moon. That gives you a complete view of where you're at with your milestones and goal progress. If you're not on track, give it another go using the full moon to set your goals to attain at the new moon, fine-tune your goals as you go along. It's also a great tool for kids who have a very different relationship with time than we do, so it makes a great tool for mutual milestone keeping — a real lunar race.

When setting goals, I like to use the SMART technique because it does the trick for me. But there are plenty of other methods you can choose from as well. Goals can be tricky, so having something to help you structure your thinking around them can be pivotal to success.

To make sure your goals are clear and reachable, make each one:

- **S**pecific (simple, sensible, significant, aligned with your North Star).
- **M**easurable (meaningful, motivating).
- **A**chievable (agreed, attainable).
- **R**elevant (reasonable, realistic, resourced, results-based).
- **T**ime-bound (time-based, time-limited, time/cost limited, timely, time-sensitive).

New Year!

You might find it strange that although I do like a party, I really dislike New Year's celebrations. The on-your-marks-get-set-GO happiness causes anxiety for me! But what I do like about New Year, and what I always pester my friends to do is to take stock and set resolutions and goals for the coming year. It's almost a bit of a fixation I think, but it's just such a perfect moment and season (element) to go within and listen. I will share an idea for a New Year ritual at the end of this chapter.

So for your first year, I'd love you to just set the goal of having fun with what you have discovered. But once you've started bedding down your lunar rhythms, you'll be in a better and more exact position to set real annual goals that you can proactively break down into smaller milestones.

To further complicate things and make them scarier, ideally, your annual goal should be guided by your seven-year goal plan. Seven YEARS! Getting vertigo? Yup, I know that feeling! But we need to be mindful and plan the first year as a dress rehearsal. Once you've established your routines and feel confident within your tree, forest, elements, North Star, and have been able to stress test your purposes and forest boundaries then it's time to explore goals in the following year/s.

As much as I might not be there with you when you've done your first year, I'd like to give a bunch of punchy questions to get your lateral thinking going. That sets the tone for long-term goal setting.

Before we do that, though, I'm going to end this chapter with my favorite quote of all time:

Twenty years from now you will be more disappointed by the things that you didn't do than by the ones you did do, so throw off the bowlines. Sail away from the safe harbor. Catch the trade winds in your sails. Explore, dream, discover. –Mark Twain

Have some fun with what you have learnt. Lean into your curiosity with gratitude and put the magic that you have found within on your proverbial mantelpiece for everybody to see and enjoy!

Lateral Thinking Questions (A Kick-Off Before You Start Setting Annual Goals)

- What are my first thoughts that come to mind about the past year? Are they positive, negative, or neutral?

- What was the most interesting thing I discovered this year?

- Who was one person I met that I'd like to get to know better, and why?

- What was my most challenging moment, and why?

- What was one of my favorite accomplishments?

- What was one personal strength I used this year, and how did I benefit from it?

- What hurdle came up repeatedly? (Time, money, approach, knowledge...)

- How well did I interact with the people who are closest to me?

- What were three accomplishments I achieved with the help of others?

- What advice would I offer someone else based on lessons I learned this year?

- What problems came up at work, and how did I solve them? Did trends become apparent on both problems and solutions?

- Who asked for my encouragement this year, and how did I help them?

- If I were writing a journal, what would I include about this year?

- What was I doing when time didn't matter, and I could just be "in the moment"?

- What frustration came up continuously?

- What did I start and not finish?

- What did I try and fail at?

- What three things do I want to learn more about?

- If I could plug-and-play mastery of one skill, what would

it be, and why?

- Who is one person that needs my help right now, and why? What would it "cost" me, and what would I gain?

- When did I slow someone else's progress? What was I apprehensive about?

- What did I make or create from scratch, and how did that make me feel?

- What experience or effort left me exhausted at the end, and how did that feel?

- What was I part of this year that I'll remember for the rest of my life, and why?

- What was the most beautiful thing anyone did for me this year?

- What was the most beautiful thing I did for another this year?

- If I could change an event or experience that happened this year, what would it be?

- What seemed difficult last year that now feels more comfortable?

- What was the best book I read this year?

- How did I deal with my thoughts and feelings? (Journaling, writing, social media, talking one-on-one with friends or family, etc.) Which method was most helpful?

- What six words best describe this year? What would I like those words to be next year?

Rabbit Hole Of Awakening

As you witnessed in the Mirror Mirror chapter, working with your own video recording can be hugely helpful. To continue with the self experimentation I want you to leave yourself an audio recording that you can listen to whenever you want to set goals or have a mindful moment about where you are on your journey.

Record your own voice or if that is too weird, ask somebody to recorded it for you.

There is a loop within the piece below that lets you choose how long you want the recording to be. Feel free to play music in the background...

Here's the text to the recording:

Choose where you want to place your attention for todays breathing moment...

... your North Star

... a specific part of your tree of life

... or a part of your forest or the boundaries that protect it

... any of the 6-elements: moon, water, earth, wind, fire, sun

... or your purpose itself...

... anything that is coming to mind at this given moment!

Wait three breaths...

make sure the motivation of the attention is playfully curious and laced with gratitude.

Wait for three breaths …

(~) Once you start to focus on the area that has been gifted your attention you will see that it will quickly start to mature into intention. What intention are you giving it? Try and be as detailed as possible.

Wait three breaths …

As the intention gathers momentum, a whole new world of insight will unfold itself in front of or within you... usually a world greater than the original.

Wait three breaths...

Again you will need to gift your attention to a specific area in this newly discovered space... gentle treading with playful curiosity and gratitude.

You lean into that new space with intent... quickly revealing the next and greater layer where you again need to choose what will receive your undivided attention with intent...

Repeat from (~) — you decide the frequency of repeat.

Close off with one minute of clear and slow belly breathing into the recording.

That is all we need to do in life!

...continuously seek where you want to put awareness, this will organically inform your attention, which naturally leans into intention...

Remember your motivation needs to be guided by self-reference and gratitude.

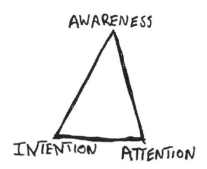

Awareness begets attention, which begets intention, which begets a new awareness within a new and greater world, and so the cycle continues...

Now THAT ladies and gentlemen is the rabbit hole of awakening!

P.S. It's also a great exercise to listen to your pilot possibly raging in protest as you do it... it's a good way to wake the pilot up again! ☺

Exercise: Identifying A Single Day's Worth Of Interconnections

Using your journal, start listing every person you interact with daily. Start with the face-to-face connections at home and work and include all the nonhumans as well. When you're done with the more obvious dealings, start adding all the people and things that weren't visible but with whom your life was connected.

For instance, if you bought a cup of coffee, you'd list the barista and cashier and then think about the people who planted, raised, picked, transported, and roasted the beans. Then add the bean plants and the place where they were cultivated. Now list the spirits of wind, water, sun, and soil that nurtured the plants. Move on to how the beans were transported to your coffee shop. Did they journey across an ocean? Imagine that trip and consider everything and everyone that was part of the journey. Move your attention to the cup. Is it paper? Where do the trees that became that paper originate? What land nurtured them? If the cup is ceramic, think about the clay soil that was transformed by the same element of fire that roasted the beans for your coffee.

Delve deeply into this exercise so that you accumulate as much detail in your notebook. Reflect on all the interdependencies that helped to make your day possible. When your day is done, breathe quietly and give thanks for all that touched your life directly and indirectly.

When you're finished, process the questions. Articulate, as best as you can, in your journal the bodily, emotional, and spiritual sensations of recognizing the breadth and depth of your interconnectedness.

How does your view of your world differ from the way you felt before this exercise? Record what you notice. .⊙.

This awareness will help you lean more into the gratitude of things that already surround you and that you can enjoy again with the wonder and amazement that we used to have when we were kids.

Building the practice of awareness allows you to become aware of where you can change, review or improve on your purpose, tree of life, forest and North Star.

New Year's Eve: 4-elements ritual

A great little activity as a group!

For every person attending, cut out of paper:

- One rectangle (from which you can fold a origami boat, if you can't do that just cut out a boat)

- Two squares

- Three hearts (on each of the three hearts put the initials of the person they are meant for, once you have done that for all of them, put them aside in a box of sorts and shake thoroughly so they can be drawn later)

- Four triangles

At the actual ceremony everybody will receive one boat, two squares, four triangles and get to pick three hearts out of the box (if they pick hearts with their own initials they should put them back and pick new ones).

Once everybody is set they should:

- (Water) Write on the boat the word that will be their North Star for the upcoming year that they want to navigate by.

- (Fire) Write down on the two squares what you don't want to carry over from the old year.

- (Wind) Write on each heart what you wish for that person whose initials are on the heart and then put them back in the box they came from.

- (Earth) Write on each triangle what you would like to manifest in the upcoming year (the triangles represent seeds)

Once everybody is done they can decide in their own time to set the boat a sail (on water close by, in a bucket, in their drink — any type of water really), burn the squares, put the hearts back into the box and go out and bury the triangles in the ground ready to grow into what you had written onto them. Ideally you should verbalize whatever is written on the paper as you execute. Once everybody is back together, start to pick out one heart at the time and read out loud (Wind) the wish written on the heart for the person in question.

AFTER THOUGHTS

My kids, although they sometimes really try to pretend that all these activity are pretty uncool, absolutely love these ritualistic elements and have learnt a lot since doing them.

The one genuinely open thing with which I can't guide my son is what the new male of the future will look like and what role he has to play in society. And it's essential that the masculine evolves and finds a place in society because without that happening the other parts of society won't be able to heal their traumas either.

Coming from the old system, I have very little advice to give beyond the obvious need to change. But I do believe that a big step towards rescuing the current situation is about reclaiming your authentic Self first.

Only if you're awakened to yourself, can you help create change because the system itself doesn't necessarily crave the change we need. Knowing the Self is all!

Learning to become aware of the Self and your surroundings takes time, and it should grow and develop organically. The good news is that you have hopefully seen that just by reading a couple of chapters and putting some intent into your purpose already, a lot of headway can be made. Bedding this down in the rhythm of the Elementalist should further help you navigate this process.

Create your own coat of arms that includes all your symbols and thoughts. Make it your own and hang it somewhere where you do a daily routine. Every year for New Year I invite you to draw a new one. Keep the old ones, so you have a witness to your self-development.

Why is it important to physically create and draw one? It's not because I am an esoteric nut job; it's because it gets things in and out of your head and anything that's out of your head will be less skewed by emotional weather and ego. It also becomes a place where you can invite other people in. More importantly, it can act as a cognitive anchoring point that can serve as a reminder in our daily routines as we're rushed off our feet; a safe harbor to anchor, to reassess and to focus.

For those of you with kids or those that feel responsible for certain youngsters within your clan and hoard, start drip-feeding these concepts to them so they can begin their journey of self-awareness. For them, it might be less of a wake-up process, and more of an urge not to FALL ASLEEP. For this please also see the follow up to this book called 'Borealis – The Forest Of Self-Discovery'.

The importance of this final chapter is to frame the journey we have been on. I still remember my panic stations about what I'm going to teach my kids during their coming-of-age chapter. Since then, I've realized that everything is currently transmuting and there is no modus operandi to hang onto really.

But what is clear is that you need to know yourself and your purpose — deeply — if you want to create something new. I love Goethe's saying that he respects the person who distinctly knows what they wish. The greater part of all mischief in the world arises from the fact that we don't sufficiently understand our own aims, yet decide to build a tower on a foundation barely deep enough to erect a hut on.

If you want to have a great life, then take great care to get to know yourself, your purpose and continue knowing yourself and your changing purpose as you evolve through life.

But as I said in the beginning, every journey starts with small steps.

With my kids, I very quickly noticed that you couldn't really drag them through the process. You'll get a sense of how much they can take in, so keep it fun and not a subscripted commitment to the Self. That's why making rituals playful is hugely important. I've been focusing on the festivals around the change of the season and walking them through which of the 6-elements they recognize in themselves and their friends, or how they can change according to the natural characteristics of the season we are about to enter. They found this very exciting and ended up creating shows that they performed at BBQs when we had the hoard over.

Realize that helping them stay awake is a constant process, and the results mustn't be programmed into them, but the awareness of the things that exist must be awakened. I was always bewildered that kids leave school knowing about syntax, elaborate math equations and the workings of volcanoes, but have no insight into what happens within their emotional landscape. With my wife being a psychotherapist, we're always baffled by this and go to great lengths to instill it in our kids.

That's one of the reasons why I created this world, Borealis - The Forest Of Self-Discovery.

Before the written word, humans as a species developed the amazing skill to process thought. We wove our wisdom and history into storytelling for the benefit and knowledge of the next generation. It was a very powerful form of communication. For example, our brain can remember a vast number composed of multiple digits if you turn the sequence of numbers into a story. We can do that without training because we're hardwired for storytelling.

So storytelling enables the drip-feeding process. That's how my kids now know that they're like a tree that stands in a magical forest surrounded by their most favorite trees and that the North Star shines exactly above where their tree stands. If they wander off too far, they will always know how to find their way back home to themselves. And yes, they also understand the four seasons, the lunar cycles and night and day. By building it all into an imaginary environment, the kids, through the power of their minds, will always have access to it, can retell it and invite other kids into this space. They also have a map to use when things get tricky, and they need to express themselves better. Whenever the time is right, we step back into the forest and learn a bit more about the Self. This also explains the esoteric overtones to these concepts.

I can't reiterate enough that this isn't about finding the result and living by it; it's about creating awareness of where one should look. The journey is the destination. We're all constantly evolving. And kids especially change at a rapid pace as they grow up. People around us change as they move through phases in their lives, and society is also evolving at a tremendous speed. As you explore your inner forest, you might see that your leaning to the elements changes, the North Star, although staying positioned in the north, might change its color. Make sure you invite the changes in and allow yourself to remain on this continuous journey as your purpose in the three parts of your forest might shift and develop over time.

From where I'm sitting as a male WEIRD tribe member, there's a lot of change ahead, including a journey of finding out what our purpose in this new world should be. We're on our own rite of passage journey. Our old narrative of what it means to be a man is dying and has to die. And as with anything in life, death can be a painful and highly unsettled time. During this process, where parts of our narrative die, vacancies appear that we feel we need to fill. It's a dangerous phase because we can fill these gaps with things that don't serve us in the long run. That's why the journey into self- discovery is so critical; it doesn't matter that you're a man; you're a person first!

Actually, this period we men are in really reminds me of being German. Especially a German growing up abroad. Wherever we went, we had the story of the Second World War hanging over us. The institutional system, to their right, were drilling everybody and anybody on how unacceptable what had happened was. It even came to a point where there were discussions about whether the local Jewish school in Johannesburg should or shouldn't sit next to us at inter-school sports events.

We're currently going through a period where a lot of fingers point towards men. And we are part of the fabric of the machine that has led us to where we are today; a world shaped by violence, exploitation and suppression. Even if it isn't of our own personal doing, it's still a heavy cross we carry and will be burdened with for years to come. It's crucial that during this time, when these cracks appear, we don't fill them with resentment, but instead find some other, more proactive way. No, unfortunately, I'm not a fortuneteller so I can't tell you how to fill these new gaps, but the one thing I'm teaching my son, who I will inevitably have to pass this burden onto is the following:

"I am a person first, and I know how I can be of service to my community through my purpose."

During my research, I stumbled across a poem that gave me a glimpse of what it could mean to be a man in the not too distant future:

The New Macho

He cleans up after himself.
He cleans up the planet.
He is a role model for young men.
He is rigorously honest and fiercely optimistic.

He holds himself accountable.
He knows what he feels.
He knows how to cry and he lets it go.
He knows how to rage without hurting others.
He knows how to fear and how to keep moving.
He seeks self-mastery.

He's let go of kidish shame.
He feels guilty when he's done something wrong.
He is kind to men, kind to women, kind to kids.
He teaches others how to be kind.
He says he's sorry.

He stopped blaming women or his parents or men for his pain
years ago.
He stopped letting his defenses ruin his relationships.
He stopped letting his penis run his life.
He has enough self-respect to tell the truth.
He creates intimacy and trust with his actions.
He has men that he trusts and that he turns to for support.

He knows how to roll with it.
He knows how to make it happen.
He is disciplined when he needs to be.
He is flexible when he needs to be.
He knows how to listen from the core of his being.

He's not afraid to get dirty.
He's ready to confront his own limitations.
He has high expectations for himself and for those he connects with.
He looks for ways to serve others.
He knows he is an individual.
He knows that we are all one.
He knows he is an animal and a part of nature.
He knows his spirit and his connection to something greater.

He knows future generations are watching his actions.
He builds communities where people are respected and valued.
He takes responsibility for himself.
In times of need, he will be his brother's keeper.

He knows his higher purpose.
He loves with fierceness.
He laughs with abandon, because he gets the joke.

Boysen Hodgson
www.mankindproject.org

This is a picture of awakened masculinity; I think a view of healthy masculinity!